GETTING READY

Helen Gilbart
Joseph Howland

FOR THE

C ollege

SECOND EDITION

L evel

A cademic

S kills

T est

H&H Publishing Company, Inc.
1117 Webb Drive
Clearwater, Florida 33515
Ph (813) 447-0835

Reading
Writing
Mathematics

Cover Art by Dorothy Thomas

Library of Congress card number 84-147966
ISBN 0-943202-13-2

Copyright 1984 by H&H Publishing Company, Inc.

All rights reserved. No part of this book may be reproduced in any
form or by any means without permission in writing from the publisher.

Printing   10   9   8   7   6   5   4   3   2

Preface

This text is designed to meet the needs of Florida's college sophomores who are preparing for the CLAST (College Level Academic Skills Test). The three chapters present, respectively, the competencies required for reading, writing, and mathematics. The communications chapters, Reading and Writing, list the competencies, explain them with examples and annotated descriptions, provide instruction for overcoming any deficiencies, and include sample tests. The chapter on Mathematics uses sample tests to illustrate and explain the computational competencies. Answers for all sample test questions are included in the respective chapters.

The book may be used by individuals or as a text for workshops. In either case, it assumes that the student needs only short-term review or instruction. Individuals with wide differences between their academic abilities and the skills demanded by the CLAST would be better served with full-course instruction on their areas of weakness.

This edition teaches the competencies as defined by the State of Florida in Summer of 1984. Future editions will aim at bringing students, instructors, and institutions the latest interpretations of the required competencies.

We wish to thank our many colleagues throughout the State of Florida who have provided support, encouragement, suggestions, and criticisms for this second edition. It is hoped that any member of Florida's academic community, students included, will continue to give us the benefit of their suggestions.

Helen Gilbart   May 1984
Joseph Howland
St. Petersburg Junior College, Clearwater Campus

TABLE OF CONTENTS

TO THE STUDENT

You have prepared yourself for test-taking and further college work by years of study in numerous courses and by your determination to succeed. The CLAST is but one more hurdle to overcome. You need to remember your preparation and prior study as you approach this test.

If you suffer from test anxiety, you can review the following points to help you get ready for the test:

The night before the test

- Be sure you know where and when the test is to be given.
- Think positively—you really are prepared due to your background and prior study in college courses.
- Make a time schedule so that you know you will have time to eat breakfast and get to the testing place without rushing.
- Get a good night's sleep.

The day of the test:

- Eat a good breakfast.

- Be sure that you have three #2 pencils and two blue or black ballpoint pens with you. (You will need the pens for the essay portion of your test.)

- Don't get to the testing place too early or too late; you will make yourself nervous by waiting around or by rushing.

- Find a good seat in the room in which the test will be given: if you like to sit near a window, in the back, or in a corner, try to seat yourself in a comfortable place.

- Do not sit with friends who may make you nervous or distracted.

- Listen carefully to the test administrator's instructions; ask questions regarding anything you do not understand.

- Survey the test carefully by reading the directions, making note of the time for each test you will take, and by looking at the answer sheets you will use.

- Plan your time well.

The test session will begin with the essay. You will be given a choice of two topics for your essay which should include an introductory paragraph, three developmental or body paragraphs, and a short conclusion. You will be given a total of fifty minutes to write the essay. Try to plan your time carefully; plan and outline your essay in about five minutes, write a smooth copy in forty minutes, and proofread for another five minutes. You will not have time to rewrite in this short time so it is important to plan and write your work as a finished copy.

After the essay-writing portion of the examination, the remainder of the test will be multiple choice questions. The reading and writing questions will be in one test booklet and timed for one hour and ten minutes. If you think that you will be able to answer the objective questions of the writing test quickly, turn to that portion first; then answer the reading test questions.

At this point in the testing, you will get a break. Be sure to walk around, eat a snack and relax during the break.

The mathematics test follows the break. It will be one hour and thirty minutes long. The test includes: arithmetic, algebra, logic, geometry, probability, statistics, and generalizations.

- Know how the test is scored.

You will not be penalized for wrong answers. Go through the test and answer the ones you are certain about first. Then look at the questions you left for further study. (You might put a question mark beside the questions you want to study. You may write in any of the test booklets.) Try to eliminate at least one or two of the answers and then make an educated guess as to which of the remaining answers is correct. Be sure to check your answer sheet so that you do not mark the wrong number. After every four or five questions, check your answer sheet number against the test booklet numbers to monitor your answers.

With a knowledge of the CLAST, your own abilities, and adequate preparation for the test, you may approach the CLAST with confidence that you will do your best. Best wishes on meeting this challenge and showing that you have mastered the competencies measured by the CLAST.

Contributed by the University of Florida

READING

The College Level Academic Skills Test is divided into three parts. The first part is essay-writing (50-minutes). The second part is the reading and writing multiple-choice Subtest (70-minutes). The reading portion of the test will be subdivided into two sections; they are: literal comprehension and critical comprehension. The third part of CLAST is the computation section (90-minutes).

This chapter begins with a listing and description of the competencies included in the reading subtest along with some instruction to further illustrate the skills and knowledge needed. The chapter ends with a sample reading test which is indicative of the type of questions that can be expected on the reading subtest.

The actual CLAST examination will have a 44 item reading subtest. Twelve of the items will test literal comprehension and the other 32 will test critical comprehension.

1

Competencies: Reading Skills

1. **Reading with literal comprehension includes all of the following skills:**

    a. **Recognize main ideas in a given passage.**

    Study this section to determine if you understand this competency:

    (1)   The main idea of a paragraph is the topic sentence; the main idea of a multi-paragraph essay is the thesis statement. Sometimes the main idea of a paragraph or essay is the first sentence. In other writings the main idea is implied, so you must understand how to pull together the ideas of the passage in order to state a main idea.

    (2)   To recognize the main idea of a passage look at the topic sentence(s). Then answer the following questions:

    (a)   What is the passage about?

    (b)   Can I state the answer to (a) in one sentence that covers the entire passage without being too broad?

    (c)   Do the supporting details of the passage all help to explain the sentence I wrote in (b)?

    b. **Identify supporting details.**

    Study this section to determine if you understand this competency:

    (1)   Supporting details help readers understand by explaining and by filling in enough information to provide a clear picture of the main idea.

(2) To identify supporting details, answer the following questions:

    (a) What is the main idea being supported?

    (b) Which sentences help readers to better understand the main idea?

    (c) Which sentences explain and fill in information related to the main idea?

    (d) Which sentences do not seem to relate to the main idea? (These sentences would not be considered supporting details; they would be vague or distracting to the unity of the passage.)

c. **Determine meaning of words on the basis of context.**

Study this section to determine if you understand this competency:

(1) Context means the surrounding words in a sentence that help determine meaning of a word.

(2) To learn the meaning of a word from its context, you should pay attention to the following:

    (a) Note the signals used to point out meaning, words such as: <u>for example</u>, <u>that is</u>, <u>another</u>, <u>this</u>, <u>that</u>, <u>these</u>, <u>those</u>, and various punctuation marks such as the colon (:) which extends an idea by making a list of examples, a dash (—) which extends an idea by using a group of words similar in meaning before and after it, and the comma (,) which marks off a synonym from the word it describes.

        Example 1. Flying mammals—millions of bats—live in the caves over there.

        Example 2. The cave was inhabited by millions of flying mammals, or bats.

        (b)   Try to paraphase sentences by restating the ideas in your own words. If you do not understand one or more words in a sentence, restate the words you do know and take an educated guess at the new vocabulary words based on your knowledge of the other words in the sentence.

    d.   **Recognize stated relationships between words, sentences, and ideas.**

       Study this section to determine if you understand this competency:

        (1)   You can recognize relationships between words by noting conjunctions like and, or, but, for, and so.

        (2)   You can determine relationships between sentences by noting the listed conjunctions as well as conjunctive adverbs like however, therefore, moreover, consequently, furthermore, and on the other hand.

        (3)   You can recognize relationships between ideas by noting the connections made for words and sentences as well as by comprehending the logical arrangement of ideas into an organized pattern such as cause-effect, time or space sequence, question-answer, or problem-solving.

2.   **Reading with critical comprehension includes all of the following skills:**

    a.   **Recognize the author's purpose.**

       Study this section to determine if you understand this competency:

        (1)   Many authors state their purpose in their thesis statements. They may use phrases like "My purpose is," or "You should understand," or "The goal of this chapter is," or "This discussion will center on." If you keep the author's purpose in mind as you read, you will better comprehend the ideas, tone, and conclusions.

(2) Other authors imply their purpose. You can
     determine the purpose by taking into consideration
     each of the topic sentences of the paragraphs of
     the passage. You can interpret the author's purpose
     by noting the progression of the author's main
     ideas as you read. Note also the tone or the
     author's attempts to influence you to feel as he or
     she feels. Authors generally try to match their
     purpose to the language they use; that is, if their
     purpose is to explain a serious issue, they use
     standard English; if their purpose is to entertain
     or to satirize, they use slang, jargon, and
     informal English to add to the effect.

b. **Distinguish between statements of fact and statements of opinion.**

   Study this section to determine if you understand this competency:

(1) A statement of fact is agreed upon evidence of
     its validity; it does not require proof to support
     it even though facts may need to be explained. If
     you said that the vernal equinox occurs on March
     21st every year, that would be an undeniable fact;
     however, you might need to explain that the vernal
     equinox is the time when the sun crosses the
     equator going in a northerly direction.

(2) A statement of opinion is the author's point of
     view, but it is not necessarily accepted or agreed
     upon by everyone. Many writers state their
     opinions and then support them with evidence in
     their effort to convince you that they are correct.
     As a reader using critical comprehension skills,
     you can analyze the author's opinions, determine
     whether or not the author's support is logical,
     complete, and valid. Then you can decide whether
     or not you agree with the author's ideas and
     opinions. If an author says that most college
     students cannot get to early classes on time, he or
     she may offer examples to support this opinion. The
     examples may cite cases of students coming in late,
     of students phoning their teachers with excuses, of
     students registering for classes beginning after 10
     a.m. If you know from your own experience that

these instances are exceptions, then you may recognize this idea as only an opinion. If, however, you have experience with college classes only in the evening, you may have to use other evidence to judge whether or not the author's opinion is valid. You might think of how many early morning classes you know to exist, how many people manage to get to work on time, and how many students you know who seem motivated to meet their responsibilities.

c.   **Detect bias and prejudice.**

Study this section to determine if you understand this competency:

(1)   Writing that is biased or prejudiced generally contains more opinion than fact. The evidence used to support the opinions may be illogical, incomplete, or invalid.

(2)   Authors expressing prejudice usually use strong, slanted, colorful language in an attempt to sway readers' opinions.

(3)   Language that contains prejudiced viewpoints may also use conditional words like <u>might</u>, <u>can</u>, <u>rather than</u>, <u>will</u>, and <u>should</u>.

(4)   Authors of prejudiced writing often use stereotypes and generalizations rather than real people and specific situations. For example, they might say, "Juvenile delinquents take law-abiding people for all they've got" instead of stating more specifically, "A sixteen-year-old male stole $25 from his neightbor."

d.   **Recognize the author's tone.**

Study this section to determine if you understand this competency:

(1)   An author's tone helps to determine the effect the writing has on the reader. Tone is the author's "voice" or attitude toward his subject.

(2) The writer's mood and attitude influence word choice, organization, selection of appropriate details and examples, and emphasis.

(3) You might describe tone in the same terms you use for descriptions of music you like:
Is it playful? Sorrowful? Down-to-earth? Highly suggestive? Symbolic?

e. **Perceive implicit as well as explicit relationships between words, sentences, and ideas.**

Study this section to determine if you understand this competency:

(1) An implicit relationship is an implied one; it involves the reader in seeing intellectual connections between words, sentences, and ideas without having them provided in the writing. An explicit relationship is a stated one; it involves the reader in understanding the relationships he or she is told in the writing.

(2) When you read, try to relate words, sentences, and ideas to what you already know. Try to read between the lines to make some mental links between ideas without requiring every idea to be stated.

f. **Recognize valid arguments and draw logical inferences and conclusions.**

Study this section to determine if you understand this competency:

(1) In order to recognize valid arguments, readers need to follow the organization from the main idea to supporting detail to facts and opinions used as examples. Does the writer use opinions only or are facts included? Does the writer assume too much or distort facts? Does the writer provide enough evidence to support the main idea? Can you, the reader, follow and agree with the conclusions?

(2) An inference calls for readers to determine meaning of an idea by reading between the lines and coming to a logical meaning. A conclusion calls for readers to put together the facts and

opinions of a passage and come to some logical resolution or ending resulting from reading.

(3) In order to draw logical inferences and conclusions, use your own past knowledge plus the new facts and opinions of the writer. Keep the main idea in mind as you read, and determine whether or not you can conclude the same ideas as those of the writer. Note the following marginal notes on the sample reading selection of several pages to help you spot examples of each of the competencies. Determine whether you can recognize any competencies not noted in the margins. As you read other selections, try to make mental notes similar to the written ones in the examples. Then you will improve your abilities to read for literal and critical comprehension. Of course, the reading you have done in college textbooks is the best preparation for achieving competency in reading. Reading improvement takes time; however, a review of the factors that make up literal and critical comprehension should assist your performance on any reading test.

Evolution of Dictionaries

Introduction

People have a vast source of material, research, and historical data at their finger-tips. A thorough knowledge of even the smallest dictionary probably classifies people as scholars, since they should be able to write and speak better than others who do not take the time to use this valuable asset to communication. However, many people take dictionaries for granted. They don't know how words get their meanings, how long words have had their present spelling and pronunciation in our language, or even how correct their dictionaries

Thesis— Main idea

are. A comparative analysis of Johnson's 1755 Dictionary of the English Language,

Thesis — Main idea

Purpose: to encourage people to learn more about dictionaries.

Webster's 1828 <u>American Dictionary of the English Language</u>, and the 1961 <u>Oxford English Dictionary</u> shows marked differences in these volumes—yet, at the time of publication, each was considered to be the best dictionary ever printed.

Supporting detail

Johnson's dictionary, which was printed in 1755, contained an awe-inspiring number of words. <u>However</u>, he allowed his personal prejudices to influence the definitions he used. His humor was shown many times in the book—<u>one example</u> being his definition of oats: "A grain, which in England is generally given to horses, but in Scotland supports the people."[1] McAdam and Milne have described Johnson's method of compiling words by saying that "there are only three ways, plus combinations, of making word-lists: recording words heard, using those in earlier dictionaries, or listing those in other books. Johnson mentions the <u>first</u> in his Preface, but dismisses it as too much work. He used the <u>second</u>, acknowledging his predecessors."[2]

Transition

Example

Prejudice and humor

Supporting detail

Example

Relationships

Facts

Supporting detail

Johnson's work on the dictionary at first was dedicated to making a complete list of all words. This book was to answer all of the questions and arbitrate all of the problems of the language, past, present, and future. Before he had worked very long, he saw that this was impossible. Johnson felt that some people were looking to his dictionary to put a stop to alterations in the language. <u>However</u>, he realized that the language would continue to grow as commerce with foreign countries increased, as people became more educated, as new sciences brought forth their own jargons, and as words were translated from one language to another.[3]

Opinion

Transition

Supporting detail · *Facts* · *Examples*

Webster's 1828 dictionary was designed to be much more complete. Webster used examples and illustrations to help his formal definitions. His spelling and pronunciation guides had many changes in them compared to the old standard English dictionaries. "Although some of the differences have grown up since Webster's day, the majority of the distinctly American spellings are due to his advocacy of them and the incorporation of them in his dictionary."[4]

Supporting detail · *Examples*

Webster felt that Americans should have their own dictionary of the English language because our form of government and our customs gave rise to new words frequently. His aim was to clarify the principles of the language, remove many of the errors, and give some regularity and consistency to the language's forms. Webster bequeathed a good standard for the people of this country, and many have copied his work. [5] — *Opinion*

Supporting detail

The OED of 1961, while much more thorough and comprehensive, still uses the same approach Webster used toward the language. — *Transition*

Facts

Of course, the OED includes many, many more words—both obsolete and slang, as well as many technical words. However, — *Transition* — the foundation or basic definitions, spelling, and pronunciation can be compared with Websters'.

Comparison

The similarities are so frequent that readers can use Webster's 1828 definitions of many common words with almost as much accuracy as they can the definitions of those same words in the OED.

Transition

Another interesting comparison between the dictionaries is to note the treatment of common words.

Extended example

Using sin (the verb) as an illustration, one can determine that there is a difference between

10

Comparison

Johnson's definitions and those of Webster. Webster encompasses a much wider area of sin than Johnson does. It leaves

Inference

one to speculate on whether Webster and Americans attributed more actions (or the lack of actions) to sin, or whether Johnson simply omitted the sin of omission as not grave enough to be classified. Perhaps offenses against society

Conclusion

and duty were not considered sins in the 18th century!

Light, humorous tone

Johnson	Webster
Sin	**Sin**
1. To neglect the laws of religion; to violate the laws of religion.	1. To depart voluntarily from the path of duty prescribed by God to man; to violate the divine law in any particular, by actual transgression or by the neglect or non-observance of its injunctions; to violate any known rule of duty.
2. To offend against right.	2. To offend against right, against men or society; to trespass.

Facts

Explicit Details

Facts

The OED devotes more than a page in its volume to the noun <u>sin</u>, and the similarity between Webster and this definition is seen again. The OED, however, adds a third definition not mentioned by the others:

Sin (noun)

1. An act which is regarded as a transgression of the divine law and an offence against God; a violation of some religious or moral principle;
2. Violation of divine law, action or conduct characterized by this; a state of transgression against God or his commands.
3. A pity; a shame. [6]

When the verb <u>sin</u> is defined, the OED uses the root word in its definition --a practice that many small pocket

11

dictionaries use, much to the consternation of their users:

Sin   (verb)
1.   To commit sin; to do a sinful act.[7]

Comparison

Both Johnson and Webster gave separate definitions for the noun and for the verb. It is easy to see that, using the third noun definition as applicable, the reader would be hard pushed to use the verb in any proper sense. "To commit a pity, a shame?" or "To do a pitiful act, a shameful act?" The user of the OED is also faced with wading through a page of examples and illustrations to ascertain just what the verb sin means--and that is both a sin and a shame!

Valid argument

Bias

Light, humorous tone

Supporting Detail

The dictionary has evolved into a marvelous collection of words and meanings as each year challenges the lexicographer to publish a newer, bigger, better book than ever before.   Readers have been amused by Johnson's definition of a lexicographer: "A writer of dictionaries; a harmless drudge, that busies himself in tracing the original, and detailing the signification of words." [8]   However, the job of lexicographers is much more complex than Johnson indicated.   They can never finish their jobs, can never feel that they have completely defined or even spelled all of the words in our language.

Opinion

Light, humorous tone

Example Bias

Transition

Implicit to the idea of the growth of language.

H. R. Warfel points out in the book, Language, A Science of Human Behavior that culture is dependent on language. "From language comes the power to shape and transmit thoughts, develop attitudes, establish beliefs, create bodies of specialized knowledge, and to train skills in making tools, instruments, machines,

Explicit list of details

Opinion

Opinion

Implicit to the idea that people still misspell and misuse words.

Transition

Conclusion

and 'all the material paraphernalia associated with living and society.' Culture, however one defines it, would be impossible without language."[9]   Fortunately, as long as society is on-going, our language will continue to be a nebulous, fluid instrument of expression.   And hopefully, lexicographers will never give up trying to trap the language on the printed page even though people pay little attention to their efforts.   If they ever stop issuing new dictionaries or defining new words, it seems reasonable to expect that society could become as dust-covered as the dictionaries found in many American homes.   Dictionaries, then, give an accurate description of the times we live in, whether changing, progressing, or slipping back.   The patterns Johnson and Webster established will not cease as long as our society advances.

End Notes

[1]E.L. McAdam, Jr. and George Milne, <u>Johnson's Dictionary</u> (New York: The Modern Library, 1965), p. 268.

[2]<u>Ibid</u>., p. viii.

[3]<u>Ibid</u>., p. 26.

[4]Albert C. Baugh, <u>A History of the English Language</u> (New York: Appleton-Century Company, 1935), p. 439.

[5]Noah Webster, <u>An American Dictionary of the English Language</u> (New York: S. Converse, 1828), preface.

[6]James Murray and others, eds., <u>The Oxford English Dictionary</u> (Oxford: Clarendon Press, 1961), pp. 69-70.

[7]<u>Ibid</u>., p. 70.

[8]Johnson, p. 233.

[9]Harry R. Warfel, _Language, A Science of Human Behavior_ (Cleveland: Howard Allen, Inc., 1962), p. 182.

Try to determine the meaning of the following words from their context:

1. Predecessors - paragraph 2

    Answer: People who lived and worked before the present time.

2. arbitrate - paragraph 2

    Answer: to settle or solve.

3. advocacy - paragraph 3

    Answer: support or consent.

4. encompasses - paragraph 5

    Answer: to enfold or cover.

5. consternation - paragraph 6

    Answer: puzzlement, confusion.

The sample reading test that begins on the following page is intended to give you a realistic experience similar to the actual CLAST Reading Test. This sample test contains 44 items which is identical to the number of items on the CLAST Reading Test. When taking the CLAST Reading Test, you will have part of the 70 minutes devoted to reading and writing test questions. It would be wise to time yourself on this sample test to evaluate your speed as well as the accuracy of your responses. Answers for this test immediately follow the test.

Reading Test

Read the following selection. Then answer the multiple-choice questions which follow it.

With the accession of Elizabeth I to the throne, a new age approached. The Renaissance, a spirit which had kindled the fires of learning in other countries, spread to England with its vibrant, intellectual queen to assist it rather than to contain or extinguish it. With Mary or sickly Edward and his protector and governor, Edward Seymour, the spirit of the Renaissance might never have spread to a receptive assemblage of subjects, and England might have continued its stifling asceticism and unproductive civil strife. Elizabeth brought not only her remarkable leadership to the throne, but also her intense desire to unify and help her people. Her education allowed her to appreciate the vitality of the times and to capitalize on it. Rather than resisting the restless individualism of the age, she nurtured it by her own unique example. The people had a woman to idolize and emulate—someone who led by ability rather than by force. And the people followed her out of gratitude and love. Writers praised Elizabeth in prose, drama, and verse, and the Queen and her subjects delighted in reading the literary homage.

Literal Comprehension:

1. The main idea of the paragraph is
   a. The Renaissance was rebirth of intellectual growth.
   b. Queen Elizabeth I helped to encourage a new age of literary brilliance.
   c. Writers praised Queen Elizabeth I in prose, drama, and verse.
   d. Queen Elizabeth I's reign was one of great leadership.

2. The Renaissance might not have spread through England if
   a. Mary or Edward had reigned.
   b. Elizabeth had not tried to read.
   c. people followed any leader.
   d. people had not tried to follow Elizabeth's example.

3. Which of these ideas is not a supporting detail in the paragraph?
   a. Elizabeth's education allowed her to encourage reading.
   b. People were inspired by Elizabeth's example.
   c. Elizabeth was an intelligent politician.
   d. England had a time of civil strife before Elizabeth came to the throne.

4. The word nurtured means
   a. encouraged.
   b. demanded.
   c. moralized.
   d. promoted.

5. The word emulate means
   a. appreciate.
   b. imitate.
   c. admire.
   d. exclude.

6. The word assemblage means
   a. every person.
   b. parts.
   c. congregation.
   d. committee.

7. Elizabeth I brought not only leadership but also what to the throne?
   a. Great reading ability.
   b. A desire to unify and help her people.
   c. Many books.
   d. Edward Seymour.

Critical Comprehension:

8. The author's purpose in this paragraph is to
   a. praise Queen Elizabeth I.
   b. show what people read in England.
   c. examine the need for leadership.
   d. tie the spread of the Renaissance to Queen Elizabeth's leadership.

9. This reading selection is composed of
    a. all facts.
    b. all opinions.
    c. a combination of facts and opinions.
    d. no opinions.

10. Would you say that the writer of the selection is
    a. giving a totally objective view of Elizabeth.
    b. showing a bias toward Elizabeth's form of leadership.
    c. prejudiced against Edward Seymour.
    d. needs more facts before judging Elizabeth's merit.

11. The author's tone in this selection is
    a. depressing.
    b. satirical.
    c. humorous.
    d. positive.

12.. The author implies that, without Elizabeth,
    a. Edward could have ruled.
    b. people would not have learned to read.
    c. literary productivity would have been less.
    d. people would have gone to war.

13. The author logically concludes that
    a. Elizabeth's examples provided people the Renaissance spirit.
    b. English people would have been conquered if Elizabeth had not reigned.
    c. people wanted more education.
    d. Elizabeth imposed her literary tastes on her subjects.

Read the following selection. Then answer the multiple-choice questions which follow it.

While the comparatively well-educated ladies of Queen Elizabeth's court sought to keep up with the learned conversations of the highly-educated and well-read courtiers, the poorly-educated, middle-class women read the more realistic, sometimes earthy, fiction of the day. There was a great interest in education for all during the later part of the sixteenth century. Richard Mulcaster and others strongly advocated education for women. Women went to elementary schools, but custom was against their attendance at advanced schools and the university. During Elizabeth's reign England may have had a higher literacy rate among women than at any time until 1850-1900. Women were educated according to position and aptitude. Many middle-class women married wealthy men as a result of their education and newly acquired social graces.[1] The humanist attitude toward education for all allowed women to learn from the Scriptures and other moral treatises. They could come closer to attainment of perfection--a humanist ideal--by reading for edification. That middle-class women branched out to the realistic fiction is no surprise. Once they learned to read English, their literary tastes were governed by the realities of sixteenth-century life as well as by the kinds of books from which they were taught. In 1579, Salter's Mirrhor of Modestie was published. It was "... designed for daughters of the growing middle class, and it dealt especially with the type of reading they should engage in. First in importance, said Salter, was Plutarch's Lives of renowned and virtuous women, and 'those of Boccaccio tending to the same,' and side by side with these accounts he placed Foxe's Book of Martyrs and the 'golden book of Erasmus dealing with the vices and virtures of the tongue.'"[2] The middle-class woman read the Bible, prayer books, devotional books and writings of early church fathers. Almanacs, popular books on medicine, cooking and

needlework were also among the books con-
sulted by housewives.[3] For women of
this social status who needed to be com-
plementary and subservient to their husbands, there could be no better reading.

Completely dominated by their fathers and
then their husbands, these hard-working
women found escape in the literature of
the time. "In spite of the classical
education of some women, there is no
doubt that the greater number were very
slightly educated, chiefly in Italian and
French, and that their taste inclined
towards a preference for slighter works,
love-poems and romances. In an early
literary work Edward Hake complains that
men bring up their daughters unwisely;
either they are 'altogether kept from
the exercises of good learning and knowledge of good letters, or else...nousled
in amourous books, vain stories, trifl-
ing fancies.' "[4] The realistic fiction
appealed to the housewives because they
could better identify with the characters
of Greene, Deloney, Rowlands, and others.
The chivalric romance seemed far-removed
from their lives. Since women's literary
taste were rather simple and prosaic, some
struggling writers tried to write about
commonplace people in a bid for this audience. A few writers, like Greene and
Lodge, wrote both romance and realistic
fiction in an effort to appeal to a wide,
varied audience. "The idealism of chivalric romance filtered into middle-class
realism.... . It was romance, with its
highly idealized heroes, that dictated
the motives of realism: the realistic
milieu and style were merely the most
effective ways of bringing their ideals
home to their audience, for while it might
have been more fun for a prentice to imagine himself a knight, it was easier for
him to envision the fruits of commercial

success. That is why, in <u>Jacke of New-berie</u>, we find a total reportorial realism surrounding the most idealized of heroes."[5]

The middle-class woman could readily imagine circumstances of <u>Thomas of Reading</u> by Deloney. The kindness of Goodwife Gray as she befriended the Earl of Shrews-bury's daughter, Margaret, was believe-able. Margaret's diligence, beauty and virtue upheld the standards of the ideal to the young woman of the tradesmen's family. The romance and adventure of the plot no doubt caused many a young maid to enjoy the story. They were able to identify with the major characters since the characters were hard-working people of low birth—a break with the character-ization of other writers.

End Notes

[1] A.L. Rouse, <u>The England of Elizabeth</u> (New York: The Macmillan Company, 1951), pp. 502-3.

[2] Lu Emily Pearson, <u>Elizabethans at Home</u> (Stanford: Stanford University Press, 1957), p. 221.

[3] Louis B. Wright, <u>Middle-Class Culture in Elizabethan England</u> (Ithaca: Cornell University Press, 1958), pp. 107-9.

[4] Phoebe Sheavyn, <u>The Literary Profession in the Elizabethan Age</u> (New York: Haskell House, 1964), p. 153.

[5] <u>Ibid.</u>, p. 154.

Literal Comprehension:

14. The main idea of the passage is that
   a. all women in the Elizabethan period were poorly educated.
   b. middle-class women of Elizabeth's time had very little education.
   c. middle-class women of the time read realistic fiction.
   d. women combined their interests with those of their husbands.

15. Sixteenth-century middle-class women read
    a. the Bible along with realistic fiction.
    b. to attain a university education.
    c. only Greek and Latin classics.
    d. romances only.

16. Writers of sixteenth-century prose
    a. wrote only to please the buyers of books.
    b. tried to adapt their fiction to the literary tastes of
       their readers.
    c. glorified romance rather than show life as it was.
    d. tried to write only about courtly love in order to capture
       middle-class women's interests.

17. The word edification in paragraph 1 means
    a. scholarship.
    b. enlightenment.
    c. pleasure.
    d. discipline.

18. The word chivalric in paragraph 2 means
    a. true.
    b. successful.
    c. down-to-earth.
    d. idealistic.

19. The word prosaic in paragraph 2 means
    a. distorted.
    b. troubled.
    c. plain.
    d. imaginary.

20. The first sentence in paragraph 1 contains
    a. a bias.
    b. a comparison.
    c. no relationships.
    d. a contradiction.

Critical Comprehension:

21. The author's purpose in writing this selection is to
    a. explain the kinds of reading of sixteenth-century middle-class women.
    b. survey the reading habits of Elizabethan women.
    c. provide a rationale for middle-class women to follow today.
    d. describe the reasons for the success of Elizabethan writers.

22. The first sentence of paragraph 2 is
    a. all facts.
    b. all opinions.
    c. part facts, part opinions.
    d. neither fact nor opinion.

23. The last sentence in paragraph 1 best illustrates
    a. a prejudice against women.
    b. a bias toward middle-class husbands who purchased good books for their wives.
    c. a prejudice against the writers of the day.
    d. a prejudice against the reading materials that kept women "in their place."

24. The author's tone is
    a. depressed.
    b. satirical.
    c. serious.
    d. sentimental.

25. The first sentence in paragraph 1 implies that
    a. the author has already discussed upper-class women's literary tastes.
    b. middle-class women read more than those at Elizabeth's court.
    c. the courtiers brought books as presents to women at Elizabeth's court.
    d. middle-class women were social climbers.

26. Paragraph 3 implies that the book Thomas of Reading provided good reading because
    a. people liked seeing how the plot progressed.
    b. it allowed young women to be thankful for their own lifestyles.
    c. women saw their own ideals in the characters.
    d. people loved stories about the upper class.

27. Readers may conclude that Salter's work described in paragraph 1
    a. dictated the literary tastes for all women.
    b. prescribed his own ideas regarding appropriate reading material for middle-class women.
    c. was prejudiced against other writers of the time.
    d. showed women how to become humanists.

28. Readers of this selection may conclude that
    a. middle-class women had an easy life.
    b. the books middle-class women were able to obtain were poorly written.
    c. middle-class women's values were reflected in their literary tastes.
    d. reading books was one way to raise a woman's social class.

Crossing the Bar

Alfred, Lord Tennyson

Sunset and evening star,
   And one clear call for me!
And may there be no moaning of the bar,
   When I put out to sea,

But such a tide as moving seems asleep,
   Too full for sound and foam,
When that which drew from out the boundless deep
   Turns again home.

Twilight and evening bell,
   And after that the dark!
And may there be no sadness of farewell,
   When I enbark;

For though from out our bourne of Time and Place
   The flood may bear me far,
I hope to see my Pilot face to face
   When I have crossed the bar.

29. The poet's main idea may be summarized by which statement?
    a. Time never stops.
    b. Evening is beautiful on a seacoast.
    c. People need guidance in order to get through life.
    d. As one dies, he or she can look forward to uniting with God.

30. The poet supports his main idea by expressing
    a. a love of nature.
    b. a trust in God.
    c. a decision to leave.
    d. a desire to return.

31. Which of the following ideas is <u>not</u> in the poem?
    a. A desire for pity.
    b. A commitment to leave willingly.
    c. A feeling of going far away.
    d. A realization of tidal action.

32. The word <u>bar</u> in this poem means
    a. hurdle.
    b. barrier.
    c. water line.
    d. beach.

33. The word <u>bourne</u> in this poem means
    a. birthplace.
    b. house.
    c. universe.
    d. stream or river.

34. The poet sees a relationship between
    a. life and nature.
    b. evening and sailing.
    c. eternity and the beach.
    d. the tides and dying.

35. The poet's purpose in the poem seems to be
    a. to warn people of death.
    b. to console friends and affirm faith.
    c. to question what will happen after death.
    d. to describe a beautiful evening of sailing.

36. The poet shows factual knowledge of
    a. tidal actions.
    b. life after death.
    c. the role of a pilot to a ship.
    d. the sinking sun.

37. The poet expresses a positive feeling for
    a. the ocean.
    b. nature.
    c. God.
    d. leaving home.

38. The tone of the poem is
    a. pessimistic.
    b. religious.
    c. morbid.
    d. sympathetic.

39. The poem connects
    a. the sun's orbit to mankind.
    b. sailing to a great adventure.
    c. the evening to a long search for God.
    d. death to a person leaving by boat.

Read the following selection. Then answer the multiple-choice questions which follow it.

Cultural expectations may have contributed or detracted from the degree to which women or men suffer from math anxiety, but both women and men frequently display behaviors that are counterproductive when interacting with mathematics. Sex roles aside, math anxiety affects a surprising cross-section of the population. Math anxiety is not limited to unsuccessful people who never completed arithmetic. Doctors, lawyers, teachers, and business executives often admit (sometimes proclaim almost proudly) to math anxiety even though they have all survived education systems and vocations which impose some mathematics requirements. More surprisingly, there are accountants and even mathematics teachers who experience incompetence when faced with some tasks that would seem easy for anyone with their occupations. For example, there is a successful accountant who never balances his own personal checking account; he relies completely on the bank statement. As another example, there is a chairperson of a mathematics department who never teaches word problems because, as she candidly admits, she "can't figure them out." The answer to the question: "Who suffers from math anxiety?" is at least 50% of the adult population, many of them in surprising occupations and positions.[1]

[1]Robert D. Hackworth, Math Anxiety Reduction (Clearwater: H & H Publishing Company, Inc., 1982), p. 4.

40. The author's purpose in writing this selection is to
   a. show why people fear math.
   b. survey the problems of learning math.
   c. show that large numbers of men and women experience math anxiety.
   d. define what people who fear math can do.

41. The author's statement that "Cultural expectations may have contributed to or detracted from the degree to which women or men suffer from math anxiety" contains
   a. all facts.
   b. all opinions.
   c. a combination of facts and opinions.
   d. neither facts nor opinions.

42. The author supports his feelings regarding the kinds of people who have math anxiety by
    a. showing how dumb at math some people are.
    b. showing that even educated people avoid certain math.
    c. expressing a prejudice toward so-called "educated" people who cannot solve math problems.
    d. expressing a bias toward people who are competent at math.

43. The author's tone is
    a. straightforward.
    b. sympathetic.
    c. alarming.
    d. slanted.

44. From reading this selection, one may conclude that
    a. people hide their weaknesses in math until they get a job.
    b. women and men need to study more math in college.
    c. more people suffer from math anxiety than any other academic problem.
    d. math anxiety, though widespread, has not kept people from becoming successful.

ANSWERS TO READING TEST

1. b	12. c	23. d	34. c
2. a	13. a	24. c	35. b
3. c	14. c	25. a	36. a
4. a	15. a	26. c	37. c
5. b	16. b	27. b	38. b
6. c	17. b	28. c	39. d
7. b	18. d	29. d	40. c
8. d	19. c	30. b	41. b
9. c	20. b	31. a	42. b
10. b	21. a	32. b	43. a
11. d	22. b	33. d	44. d

Contributed by Florida State University

WRITING

WRITING INTRODUCTION

The writing competencies included in the College Level Academic Skills Test may be divided into two categories. In the first category the competencies include skills in (1) word choice, (2) sentence structure, and (3) grammar, spelling, and punctuation. There are 36 test items in this category with six for word choice, ten for sentence structure, and 20 for grammar, spelling, and punctuation. Students will have 30 minutes to complete this section.

A second category for writing competencies requires a writing sample. Fifty minutes will be provided for the generation of a four to six paragraph essay on a selected topic. Two topics will be given on the test, and the student must write the essay on one of the two topics.

This chapter begins with a listing and description of the writing competencies along with some instruction to further illustrate the skills and knowledge needed. The chapter ends with two sample 36-item writing tests on the broad skills area. Answers follow each test.

Competency III: Writing Skills

Sub–Competency A

Compose units of discourse which provide ideas and information suitable for purpose and audience and which include all of the following skills:

1. **Select a subject which lends itself to expository writing.**

    Study this section to determine if you understand this competency.

    a. Note the four types of writing:
        Narration = tells a story
        Description = paints a word picture of a person,
                           place, or object
        Argumentation = attempts to convince or sway the
                              reader's opinion
        Exposition = explains ideas or information

    b. Study the list of subjects and select the ones that
        would be appropriate for an expository essay.
        Selection of a New Car*   A Day at the Beach
        An Unforgettable Incident   Bringing Up Children Today
        Legalized Gambling   Living in Florida*
        Career Choices*   My Bedroom Sanctuary
        Restricting Gun Control Laws*
        Influences of Television*
        Choosing a Major Area for Study*

*The starred items lend themselves to exposition. Of course, you could also write a paper using narration, description, or argumentation on the starred topics; however, if you remember that you are trying to select a subject by which you can explain your ideas and provide information to the reader, you will be able to use any of the starred topics.

2. **Determine the purpose for writing.**

   Study this section to determine if you understand this competency.

   a. You should be certain of just what the assignment is asking you to do. If it requires you to write an expository essay, then you know that your purpose is to explain your ideas.

   b. You should aim your explanations at a general reading audience, not a teacher, testmaker, employer, or friend. Use standard English which will be acceptable to anyone who reads your writing. Assume that your reader is neither totally ignorant nor completely informed on your topic. Make sure that you provide enough information and examples to make the average reader understand your ideas.

3. **Limit the subject of a topic to one which can be developed within the requirements of time, purpose, and audience.**

   Study this section to determine if you understand this competency.

   a. If you are given 50 minutes to write the essay, be sure that you use your time well. Restrict and plan your essay for about 5 minutes; write as clearly as possible on the paper provided for about 40 minutes; then revise, proofread, and make corrections to the essay for 5 minutes.

   b. If you fail to plan adequately, your essay may become a jumble of disjointed, poorly organized facts. If you fail to save time for revising and proofreading, readers of your essay may find numerous careless errors, omissions of words, and errors of punctuation and spelling which detract from the overall explanation of your ideas.

   c. Plan on an introductory paragraph (50 - 75 words) with your thesis statement at the end of it, three developmental paragraphs (150 words each), and a concluding paragraph (35 - 50 words) for a total of about 500 - 600 words.

   d. Using one of the starred topics on the previous list, practice limiting a topic to one appropriate for a short expository essay.

Example: Career Choices

You cannot begin to cover the entire topic; in fact, you could write a book on career choices in health care, business, engineering, education, etc.

Use the topic to brainstorm and limit your ideas:

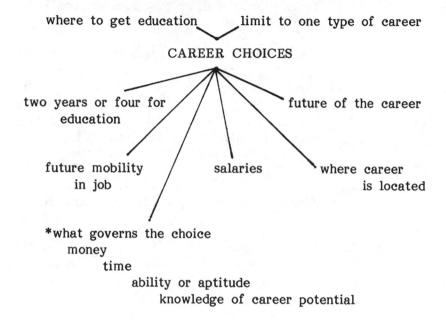

where to get education   limit to one type of career

CAREER CHOICES

two years or four for
education

future of the career

future mobility
in job

salaries

where career
is located

*what governs the choice
   money
       time
           ability or aptitude
               knowledge of career potential

e.   Note that in the brainstorming to limit the topic, you write many ideas. Some are too vague to pursue; others require information that you may not have without doing research.   Keep writing limited topics until you think of one that lends itself to a 500 - 600 word expository essay. Write ways to break that topic into logical parts that cover your restricted topic <u>without overlapping</u>.   Write as many subtopics as you know you can explain without wandering into areas of the subject that will require too much explanation for the time allotted.

f.   Remember that the testmakers will provide a topic that any sophomore student should be able to explain, so do not feel that you will not be able to write this important essay. Make up your mind to do your best with the topic and the time, and you will be able to write a successful essay.

4. **Formulate a thesis statement which reflects the purpose.**

    Study this section to determine if you understand this competency.

    a. A thesis statement states the controlling or main idea of a multi-paragraph essay. It explains in one concise statement what the reader can expect to learn from reading the essay.

    b. The thesis statement is the most important sentence in an essay; therefore, you should plan its parts carefully:

        Restricted subject + active voice verb + specific information regarding each of the developmental paragraphs.

        Example:

        Restricted subject   Active voice verb

        A student planning a
        career in computer science   needs

        Specific information for three paragraphs

        enough money to pay for education,
        an aptitude for working at a highly organized job,
        and knowledge of future career responsibilities.

    c. Remember that the parts of the thesis statement which help the reader understand the main idea of the essay are the specific ideas that you plan to develop in your paragraphs. Do not trap yourself into becoming repetitious by making two of those parts overlap so that you must cover the same information twice.

5. **Develop the thesis statement by all of the following:**

    a. **Provide adequate support which reflects the ability to distinguish between generalized and concrete evidence.**

        Study this section to determine if you understand this competency.

        Try to be as specific as you can. Eliminate or define words like <u>factors</u>, <u>things</u>, <u>advantages</u>, <u>today's society</u>, and <u>characteristics</u> so that your reader receives your exact information without having to guess what you mean.

Example: A student needs to remember several things regarding educational factors.

This sentence is vague and general. You can re-write it by using concrete, specific word choice:
A student needs to remember the amount of time, money, and effort required for a two-year degree program in computer science.

b. Arrange the main ideas with supporting details in an organizational pattern appropriate to the expository purpose.

Study this section to determine if you understand this competency.

(1) Note the arrangement of the parts of the sample thesis statement:
A student planning a career in computer science needs enough money for education, an aptitude for working at a highly organized job, and knowledge of future career responsibilities.

(2) Note that the parts are arranged in logical order:
first, get the money for education;
next, find out if you have the aptitude to do highly organized work;
last, learn future responsibilities of the career.

(3) You should also make a rough outline of your supporting details for each point. The easiest and most common pattern of organization is as follows:
Thesis Statement
I. Topic sentence = first part of thesis
   A. Supporting detail
      1. Example
      2. Example
   B. Supporting detail
      1. Example
      2. Example
   C. Supporting detail
      1. Example
      2. Example
II. Topic sentence = second part of thesis
   A. Supporting detail
      etc.

34

(4)   If you follow your outline as you write, you will develop and explain your topic fully and clearly.

c.   **Write unified prose in which all supporting material is relevant to the thesis statement.**

Study this section to determine if you understand this competency.

As a writer of unified prose, you should stick to the point. Do not wander off to a related topic. If you look at the brainstorming on the topic "Career Choices," you will see many interesting ideas; however, you should use only the ideas that develop what you promised to explain to the reader in the thesis statement. Never pad an essay with other information on a related subject because you will lead the reader away from the topic by your lack of unity.

d.   **Write coherent prose, providing effective transitional devices which clearly reflect the organizational pattern and the relationships of each part.**

Study this section to determine if you understand this competency.

(1)   Coherent paragraphs contain writing that flows smoothly from main idea to supporting detail to example. The writer leads the reader along with logical organization, repetition of key words, repetition of ideas through parallel structure, and transitional devices.

(2)   Note the use of coherence devices in the following sample paragraph:

In addition to the money needed for education and the aptitude for highly organized work, students who plan careers in computer science must understand future responsibilities of the career. They must realize that employees who work with computers need additional training throughout their work lives. They can look forward to learning to use new technology as it evolves. New employees might work with a computer with twice the capabilities of the one they first used in college. As they learn, computer science students may also want to take computer management courses so they can advance within an industry. For example, students with background in management can look forward to moving up from programmers to systems analysts to managers of computer units. They can advance as their college training and aptitudes allow. Another part of future job responsibilities a computer science student must consider is travel. Some students may prefer to stay in one location rather than to travel as some large industries require. Other students may like the idea of travelling to other cities to work at different computer installations. They may be able to select a job with a company that provides travel in California, New York, or even overseas. If students feel competent to handle these future career requirements, they will work hard in college so they can join an industry that allows them to reach their goals.

Sub-Competency B

Transmit ideas and information in effective writing language which conforms to the conventions of standard American English. This includes all of the following skills:

1. **Demonstrate effective word choice by all of the following skills:**

   a. **Use words which convey the denotative and connotative meaning required by context.**

      Study this section to determine if you understand this competency:

      (1) Read each example carefully, and try to determine its meaning.

      (2) Look at the words which seem to be important to understanding the sentence. Do they seem appropriate to the message of the sentence? Are the words correct for the exact meaning intended (the denotative meaning) or do any words carry emotional associations (the connotative meaning)?

36

(3)   Study the following examples and their corrections:

Example 1.   Martin has the addiction of biting his fingernails.

Martin has the habit of biting his fingernails.

Example 2.   She gave the teacher a copout for missing the last three days.

She gave the teacher an excuse for missing the last three days.

Example 3.   The horses pulling the wagon were great big, enormous stallions.

The horses pulling the wagon were enormous.

Example 4.   Murphy's Law is a principal I've found to be true.

Murphy's Law is a principle I've found to be true.

Example 5.   We were already to go when we were told that the flight was cancelled.

We were all ready to go when we were told that the flight was cancelled.

b. **Avoid slang, jargon, cliches, and pretentious expressions.**

Study this section to determine if you understand this competency:

(1) Read each example carefully and try to determine its meaning.

(2) Look for words that may be examples of slang (unconventional colorful language invented for specific uses), jargon (language of a trade or profession), cliches (overused phrases), or pretentious expressions (unnecessary use of ornate language).

(3) Study the following examples:

Example 1. We hit the sack early because we had a long hike the next day.

We went to bed early because we had a long hike the next day.

Example 2. Try to finalize your plans by 3:00 p.m.

Try to finish your plans by 3:00 p.m.

Example 3. I was completely pooped when I finished the race.

I was exhausted when I finished the race.

Example 4. The plane disappeared from view, so we thought it had crashed.

The plane disappeared, so we thought it had crashed.

Example 5. Last but not least, don't gab about areas of linguistic sophistication about which you know zilch.

Last, don't talk about areas of linguistic sophistication about which you know nothing.

c. **Avoid wordiness.**

Study this section to determine if you understand this competency:

(1) Read each sentence carefully, and try to determine its meaning.

(2) Attempt to cut some of the wordiness to make a more concise sentence without losing the meaning.

(3) Study the following examples.

Example 1. I don't have much money at this point in time.

I don't have much money now.

Example 2. I personally feel that pictures of dead bodies should not be in the newspapers.

I feel that pictures of bodies should not be in the newspaper.

Example 3. Using cake batter that is green in color is a new innovation.

Using green cake batter is an innovation.

Example 4.   His plan entirely eliminated the need to surround the troops on all sides.

His plan eliminated the need to surround the troops.

Example 5.   In this day and age, many people continue on with their education.

Today, many people continue their education.

2.   **Employ conventional sentence structure by all of the following:**

a.   **Place modifiers correctly.**

Study this section to determine if you understand this competency:

(1)   Read each example carefully, noting the way each correction is made.   Modifiers need to be placed near the words they describe, so most corrections involve clarifying the sentence by putting these parts closer together.

Example 1.   The graceful black cat followed the boy with a red collar and a white spot on its throat.

The graceful black cat with a red collar and a white spot on its throat followed the boy.

Example 2.   Chairs and tables are being furnished to the drama club with plastic tops.

Chairs and tables with plastic tops are being furnished to the drama club.

Example 3. Walking down the street, the gardens looked lovely.

As I was walking down the street, I saw that the gardens looked lovely.

Example 4. She studied all evening and almost made a grade on the test as high as her friend's.

She studied all evening and made a grade on the test almost as high as her friend's.

Example 5. Mark told of his overseas flight in the first paragraph of his paper.

Mark told in the first paragraph of his paper about his overseas flight.

b. **Coordinate and subordinate sentence elements according to their relative importance.**

Study this section to determine if you understand this competency:

(1) Read each example carefully, noting the appropriate order of the sentence parts.

(2) Determine which sentence part contains the more important idea; then subordinate the other idea.

Example 1. Beethoven is a German composer, and he is best known for his nine symphonies.

Beethoven, a German composer, is best known for his nine symphonies.

Example 2. The film "Reds" will be shown Saturday. It will be in the auditorium at 8:00 p.m.

The film "Reds" will be shown Saturday at 8:00 p.m. in the auditorium.

Example 3. Burning the entire second floor, the fire started at midnight.

The fire which started at midnight burned the entire second floor.

Example 4. Though we have had rain for seven days, the rainfall for August is normal.

The rainfall for August is normal even though we have had rain for seven days.

Example 5. The boat overturned yesterday when five men drowned.

Five men drowned yesterday when the boat overturned.

c. **Use parallel expressions for parallel ideas.**

Study this section to determine if you understand this competency:

(1) Read each example carefully, noting the two or three sentence parts. When describing or discussing two or more ideas, each part should be written in a similar or parallel way.

(2) If you isolate each idea, you can easily correct each sentence.

Example 1. I like reading, writing, and to swim in the lake.

I like (1) reading,
       (2) writing,
       (3) swimming in the lake.

Example 2. Mary is talented, bright, and thinks she will be a lawyer.

Mary is (1) talented and (2) bright; (3) she thinks she will be a lawyer.

Example 3. The team has always shown great respect and love of the traditions at Homecoming.

The team has always shown (1) great respect for and (2) love of the traditions at Homecoming.

Example 4. Most students have the choice of vacationing or to go to summer school.

Most students have the choice of (1) vacationing or (2) going to summer school.

Example 5. The anthropologist spent a year in the desert, in the Alaskan wilderness, and the jungle looking for primitive tribes.

The anthropologist spent a year (1) in the desert, (2) in the Alaskan wilderness, and (3) in the jungle looking for primitive tribes.

d. Avoid fragments, comma splices, and fused sentences.

Study this section to determine if you understand this competency:

(1)   Read each example carefully, noting that each complete thought or independent clause must be set off by appropriate punctuation.

(2)   A fragment is only part of a complete sentence; a comma splice incorrectly joins two independent clauses with a comma; a fused sentence incorrectly runs two independent clauses together without punctuation.

Example 1. People trying to buy homes today with the interest rates as high as they are.
(Fragment: sentence has no verb.)

People still try to buy homes today even though interest rates are high.

43

Example 2. Try to use all of your skills on the team, you may make the first team.
(comma splice)

Try to use all of your skills on the team, and you may make the first team.

Example 3. The police found the lost boy he was asleep under a tree.
(fused sentence)

The police found the lost boy; he was asleep under a tree.

Example 4. It rained all day, consequently we had to postpone the picnic.
(comma splice)

It rained all day; consequently, we had to postpone the picnic.

Example 5. Although he was unable to vote because he had failed to register.
(fragment)

Although he was unable to vote because he had failed to register, he still followed the election closely.

3. **Employ effective sentence structure by all of the following:**

   a. **Use a variety of sentence patterns.**

   Study this section to determine if you understand this competency:

   (1) Read the examples which make use of varied sentence patterns.

   (2) Try writing sentences of your own, using the same patterns.

   Example 1. The concert kept my attention throughout the evening.
   (Simple sentence)

Example 2.   The music played was my favorite, and the orchestra was the largest in Florida.
(Compound sentence)

Example 3.   I had studied the symphony notes before I went to the concert.
(Complex sentence - dependent clause last)

Example 4.   Even though I knew little classical music, I appreciated Bach's compositions very much.
(Complex sentence - dependent clause first)

Example 5.   As long as children anywhere in the world are deprived of learning about music, as long as any adults are restricted in the music they can listen to, we cannot say we are free.
(Periodic sentence - main idea last)

b.   **Avoid unnecessary use of passive construction.**

Study this section to determine if you understand this competency:

(1)   Study the examples carefully, noting that verbs should be changed to the active voice.

(2)   This change usually involves putting the subject or the doer of the action in front of the verb. The verb form then becomes present or past tense rather than present or past participle.

Example 1.   Your registration has been cancelled and your money refunded.

We have cancelled your registration and refunded your money.

Example 2.   The dog had been bathed by the boy, but its coat still looked dirty.

The boy bathed the dog, but its coat still looked dirty.

45

Example 3.   The game had been lost, so the team spirit had been dampened.

The team's loss of the game dampened their spirits.

Example 4.   The new coat was worn by mother.

Mother wore the new coat.

Example 5.   You should remember that bills must be paid, phone calls made on time, and letters written in good form.

You should remember to pay your bills, make phone calls on time, and write letters in good form.

c.   **Avoid awkward constructions.**

Study this section to determine if you understand this competency.

(1)   Study the examples, noting that most awkward constructions can be smoothed out by editing and by cutting down on the number of words in the sentence.

(2)   Write and revise some of your own sentences.

Example 1.   Being that I am only 18, I haven't considered marriage very seriously.

Since I am only 18, I haven't considered marriage very seriously.

Example 2.   The reason is because I have my education to complete.

The reason is that I have my education to complete.

Example 3.   When only a small boy, my house burned to the ground.

When I was only a small boy, my house burned to the ground.

46

Example 4. Winning the prize is where he must make no mistakes all day.

To win the prize, he must make no mistakes all day.

Example 5. When a runner wears improper shoes, it causes him to get injured.

Wearing improper shoes causes a runner injuries.

4. **Observe the conventions of standard American English grammar and usage by all of the following:**

   a. **Use standard verb forms.**

      Study this section to determine if you understand this competency.

      (1) Read each example carefully, noting the correction in the verb forms.

      (2) Use a handbook or dictionary to help you determine the principal parts of verbs about which you feel unsure.

      (3) Use the following patterns to determine principal parts of verbs:

      I _____ today. = present tense
      I _____ yesterday. = past tense
      I have _____ every day. = past participle

      Examples:

present	drive	go	do
past	drove	went	did
past participle	driven	gone	done

      Example 1. The speaker inferred that the audience was stupid.

      The speaker implied that the audience was stupid.

Example 2. She use to come to see our family, and she ask us to visit her home in the mountains.

She used to come to see our family, and she asked us to visit her home in the mountains.

Example 3. Don't let that terrible site effect your plans to go on alone.

Don't let that terrible sight affect your plans to go on alone.

Example 4. They shouldn't of past that gas station because it was the last one for fifty miles.

They shouldn't have passed that gas station because it was the last one for fifty miles.

Example 5. If you loose the game, everyone will go to the tournament accept you.

If you lose the game, everyone will go to the tournament except you.

b.   **Maintain agreement between subject and verb.**

Study this section to determine if you understand this competency:

(1)   In clauses or sentences a verb must agree with its subject in person (1st, 2nd, 3rd person) and number (singular or plural).

(2)   In the following examples note the subjects and verbs.

(3)   Do not be distracted from finding subjects by prepositional phrases between the subject and verb.

In the following examples all subjects are in bold face print; all verbs are underlined.

48

Example 1. **Mary** and **John** <u>need</u> help with writing.

Example 2. There <u>are</u> a **couch,** three **chairs,** and two **tables** in the living room.

Example 3. The new **gym** with its exercise equipment, indoor track, and handball court <u>fills</u> a great need in our community.

Example 4. **Everyone** who loves folk music <u>wants</u> to attend.

Example 5. The **scissors** <u>are broken.</u>

c. Maintain agreement between pronoun and antecedent.

(1) An antecedent is a noun or pronoun which is referred to later in the sentence as a pronoun. Singular antecedents require singular pronouns to be used; plural antecedents require plural pronouns.

(2) Read the examples carefully, noting the antecedents which are underlined.

Example 1. <u>Everyone</u> must do their work.

Correction: <u>Everyone</u> must do his work.

Example 2. <u>Many</u> of the students were trying to answer his study questions.

Correction: <u>Many</u> of the students were trying to answer their study questions.

Example 3. Neither <u>John</u> nor <u>Mark</u> has completed their study of English.

Correction: Neither <u>John</u> nor <u>Mark</u> has completed his study of English.

Example 4. Either the <u>coach</u> or the <u>players</u> can set the argument straight by telling his opinion.

Correction: Either the <u>coach</u> or the <u>players</u> can set the argument straight by telling their opinions.

Example 5. The <u>group</u> is planning their picnic.

Correction: The <u>group</u> is planning its picnic.

d. **Use proper case forms.**

Study this section to determine if you understand this competency:

(1) English pronoun forms must be used consistently to show either the subjects of sentences, to show possession, or to stand for the object of a verb or preposition.

Cases	Singular	Plural
Subjects	I, you, he, she, it	we, they, who
Possessives	my, mine, your, our	their, whose
Objects	me, you, him, her, it	us, them, whom

(2) Determine the way the pronouns are being used in the following examples. Keep in mind that only those pronouns may be used that fit by case into the structure of the sentence.

(3) In the examples in which compound subjects or objects are used, you may subtract one and then the other, and the appropriate case will become obvious.

Example: To decide if the sentence "John and me are going to the movies." is correct first write the following two sentences:
John is going to the movies.
Me are going to the movies.
The second sentence obviously is not correct and should be changed to:
I am going to the movies.
Therefore, a correct sentence for the original idea is:
John and I are going to the movies.

Note the following examples and corrections.

Example 1. The movies made mother and I cry.

The movies made mother and me cry.

Example 2. Both Mary and her have read the play.

Both Mary and she have read the play.

Example 3.   Several of we singers have sore throats.

Several of us singers have sore throats.

Example 4.   Us students won't put up with that rule.

We students won't put up with that rule.

Example 5.   My brother is two years older than me.

My brother is two years older than I am.

e.   **Maintain a consistent point of view.**

Study this section to determine if you understand this competency:

(1)   You need to maintain the same point of view by avoiding shifts in numbers (singular plural), tense (present, past), voice (active, passive), or person (1st, 2nd, 3rd).

(2)   Study the examples carefully, noting the way needless shifts are corrected.

Example 1.   He goes up on the porch and rang the bell.

He went up on the porch and rang the bell.

Example 2.   The dog loved steak, and even the bones were enjoyed.

The dog loved steak and even enjoyed the bones.

Example 3.   Students have studied until you know how to take the test.

Students have studied until they know how to take the test.

51

Example 4. Each player must try their best.

Each player must try his or her best.

Example 5. Pour two cups of flour into a bowl, and then the cook adds a cup of milk.

The cook pours two cups of flour into a bowl and then adds a cup of milk.

5. **Use standard practice for spelling, punctuation, and capitalization.**

   Study this section to determine if you understand this competency:

   a. Study lists of frequently misspelled words in handbooks and English composition texts. The following list will help you get started:

1. accommodate	18. benefit	32. definite
2. accidental	beneficial	definitely
accidentally	19. busy	definition
3. acquaint	business	define
acquaintance	20. category	33. describe
4. acquire	21. cemetery	description
5. address	22. choose	34. disastrous
6. advice	chose	35. distress
advise	choice	36. embarrass
7. affect	23. comparative	37. environment
effect	24. conscientious	38. equipped
8. all right	conscience	equipment
9. ambitious	conscious	39. exaggerate
10. among	consciousness	40. excellent
11. analyze	25. consistent	excellence
analysis	consistency	41. exist
12. apparent	26. control	existence
13. appear	controlled	existent
appearance	controlling	42. experience
14. argument	27. controversy	43. explanation
arguing	controversial	44. familiar
15. athlete	28. course	45. fascinate
16. began	coarse	46. forty
begin	29. criticism	fourth
beginner	criticize	47. general
beginning	30. decision	48. government
17. belief	decided	governor
believe	31. defendant	

49. grammar
    grammatically
50. height
51. history
52. imagine
    imaginary
    imagination
53. immediate
    immediately
54. impressionable
55. incident
    incidentally
56. independence
57. indict
58. initial
59. intelligent
    intelligence
60. interest
61. interpret
    interpretation
62. irrelevant
63. its
    it's
64. laboratory
65. led
66. library
67. license
68. loneliness
    lonely
69. loose
    lose
    losing
70. marriage
71. mathematics
72. necessary
    unnecessary
73. Negro
    Negroes
74. noticeable
    noticing
75. occasion
76. occur
    occurred
    occurring
    occurrence

77. opportunity
78. origin
    original
79. passed
    past
80. perform
    performance
81. personal
    personnel
82. playwright
83. possess
    possession
84. practical
85. precede
86. prefer
    preferred
87. prejudice
88. prepare
89. prevalent
90. principal
    principle
91. privilege
92. probably
93. proceed
    procedure
94. professor
    profession
95. prominent
96. psychology
    psychoanalysis
    psychopathic
    psychosomatic
97. pursue
98. really
    realize
99. receive
    receiving
100. recommend
     recommendation
101. referring
102. repetition
     repetitious
103. responsible
104. rhythm
105. selected

106. seminar
107. sense
108. separate
     separation
109. shining
110. similar
111. sophomore
112. studying
113. success
     succeed
     succession
     successful
114. surprise
115. temperature
116. than
     then
117. their
     there
     they're
118. thorough
119. tries
     tried
120. too
     to
     two
121. useful
     useless
     using
122. usual
     unusual
123. varies
     various
124. vicious
125. weather
     whether
126. woman
127. write
     writing
     writer

b. Review rules that govern the spelling of many commonly used words.

    (1)   Write i before e except after c if the sound of the two letters is the long e (ē). If the sound is not ē, use ei. Examples of this rule:
        receive, foreign, weigh, relief, field.

    (2)   When adding a suffix to a word, except "ing," change y to i in most cases.
        Examples of this rule are:
          happy + ness = happiness
          study + ing = studying
          accompany + ed = accompanied
          carry + ing = carrying
          carry + ed = carried

    (3)   When forming the plural of many words, add s except when the pronunciation of the plural adds a syllable to the word; then add es.
        Examples of this rule:
        adolescents, calendars, approaches, watches

    (4)   When adding a suffix, double the final consonant if the consonant is preceded by a single vowel and if the consonant is the last letter of an accented syllable.
        Examples of this rule:
        referring, benefited, allotted, beginning, admittance

c. Study common punctuation rules.

    (1)   Use a comma between introductory clauses joined by coordinating conjunctions (and, but, or, nor, for, so).

        Example: We wanted to see the show, but we didn't get there on time.

    (2)   Use a comma between introductory elements and the rest of the sentence.

        Example: After I graduate from college, I plan to go to graduate school.

(3)   Use a comma between items in a series.

>   Example: A good teacher is well organized, knowledgeable, and interested in students.

(4)   Use a comma to set off explanatory or parenthetical parts of a sentence.

>   Example: The meeting, for your information, will begin at 9:00 a.m.

(5)   Use a comma between addresses and dates and the read of the sentence.

>   Example: He vacationed at the White Pine Hotel, 98 Ashland Street, Radford, Virginia, in May, 1984.

(6)   Use a comma to separate a direct quotation from the rest of the sentence.

>   Example: "Call the police," she screamed, "and tell them to come quickly!"

(7)   Use a comma between contrasting parts of a sentence.

>   Example: It was John, not Harry, who paid for our dinner.

(8)   Use a comma between nonrestrictive words, phrases, and clauses and the rest of the sentence.

>   Example: She is as tall as, though two years younger than, her brother.

(9)   Use a semicolon between parts of sentences which already contain commas.

>   Example: The starting lineup includes Mary Gardner, forward; Jean Phillips, center; and Helen Weaver, guard.

(10)   Use semicolons between independent clauses if
either clause contains other commas.

  Example: She is a beautiful, talented, young
      woman; but she will have trouble getting
      to Hollywood, New York, or Boston
      because of her attitude.

(11)   Use semicolons between independent clauses joined
by a conjunctive adverb such as <u>however</u>, <u>there-</u>
<u>fore</u>, <u>moreover</u>, <u>furthermore</u>, <u>consequently</u>, or <u>on</u>
<u>the</u> <u>other</u> <u>hand</u>.

  Example; The test began on time; however, we
      were late getting out of class.

(12)   Use a colon before a list.

  Example: The following students will audition
      for the play: John, Cynthia, Ted, Nadine,
      and Terry.

(13)   Use a colon after a formal quotation.

  Example; Patrick Henry made his stand very clear:
      "Give me liberty, or give me death."

(14)   Use a colon before an explanation or example.

  Example: The course gave me a great deal of
      trouble: hundreds of pages of read-
      ing, many papers, and essay tests.

(15)   Use a colon before a long question.

  Example: The jurors knew that they had a
      difficult problem to solve: Was the
      accused at the scene of the crime or
      was his shaky alibi believable?

(16)   Capitalize the first word of every sentence, even
a quotation within a sentence.

  Example: The president said, "I will try to
      gain consensus and report to you the
      next meeting."

(17) Capitalize proper nouns such as names and titles of people

   Example: President Reagan, Tiny Tim, The Supremes, Phyllis Diller.

(18) Capitalize proper nouns such a regions of the country.

   Example: The North, Southwest, Southern California.

(19) Capitalize proper nouns such as names of places, holidays, specific dates.

   Example: Florida, New Year's Day, Epcot Center, the Romantic Period.

(20) Capitalize countries, races, and languages.

   Example: Japanese, English, Caucasian, Mexico.

(21) Capitalize names of businesses and organizations.

   Example: Central Baptist Church, Times Square Shopping Center, Islam, Florida Education Association.

(22) Capitalize names of college courses if they are specific; do not capitalize if they are general names of classes.

   Example: sociology, Sociology 2450, Biology 1130, French, physical education.

(23) Capitalize the first letter of each word in titles of books, poems, songs; do not capitalize an article or preposition unless it is the first word of the title.

   Example: "The Song of the South," King Lear, Fiddler on the Roof.

6. **Revise, edit, and proofread units of written discourse to assure clarity, consistency, and conformity to the conventions of standard American English.**

   Study this section to determine if you understand this competency.

   a. Look for errors of word choice, grammar, spelling, punctuation, and capitalization in your own writing when you proofread; then revise carefully.

   b. Use the list of competencies you have just studied as a guide or check list in order to find errors.

Two sample writing tests follow this paragraph. They are intended to give you a realistic experience similar to the actual CLAST examination on the broad skill areas of writing. Each sample test contains 36 items. You have approximately 35 minutes to complete the test. It would be wise to time yourself on these sample tests to evaluate your speed as well as the accuracy of your responses. Each test has answers immediately following.

WRITING TEST A

Multiple Choice: Select the best answer. Do not mark more than one answer.

Directions: Complete each sentence by choosing the most effective word or phrase which conforms to standard written English.

1. They wanted to_____balance.

      a. verify and check their account
      b. check out the leftover
      c. check their account
      d. tally up the remaining

2. They _____with the confidence that they would win.

      a. sauntered toward the gaming house
      b. hoofed it over to the gambling parlor
      c. traveled to the house for games of chance
      d. walked to the gambling house

Writing

3. The astronauts _____ their trip into space with a celebration.

   a. finalized
   b. finished off
   c. terminated
   d. ended

4. George _____ car accident.

   a. perished in the catastrophic
   b. died in the terrible
   c. was found to have lost his life in the
   d. was deceased after the awful

5. _____, people must realize their responsibilities to animals.

   a. To conclude
   b. Lastly
   c. Last but not least
   d. In the final analysis

6. The woman's ideas on space travel _____.

   a. were hailed as totally unique
   b. were prioritized at the top
   c. were judged to be very unique
   d. were praised as unique

7. When I walked home, _____.

   a. I noticed that the grass needed cutting
   b. the grass needed cutting
   c. the cutting of the grass was the first thing I noticed
   d. the need to cut the grass was noticed by me

8. The teacher lectured _____

   a. to our class which was boring and poorly organized.
   b. which was boring and poorly organized to the class.
   c. in a boring, poorly organized way to the class.
   d. to the class in a boring, poorly organized way.

9. The student was _____ regarding his plans after graduation.

      a. on the fence
      b. undecided
      c. up in the air
      d. unable to make a decision

10. She decided to _____ the game because she enjoyed it so much.

      a. continue on with
      b. repeat again
      c. keep on with
      d. continue

Directions: Choose the sentence that expresses the thought most clearly and effectively and that has no errors in structure.

11. I did not know whether _____

      a. I should go to the university of if I should get a job.
      b. I should go to the university or get a job.
      c. to go to the university or if I should get a job.
      d. to go to the university or whether I should get a job.

12.
      a. I hit that ball, and I hit a home run.
      b. When I hit that ball, it was a homerun.
      c. I hit a homerun when I hit that ball.
      d. I hit that ball, so it was a homerun.

13.
      a. Bills should be paid, vacation funds saved, and contributions made to charity.
      b. You should pay your bills, save vacation funds, and contributions should be made to charity.
      c. You should pay your bills, vacation funds should be saved, and contributions made to charity.
      d. Pay your bills, save vacation funds, and make contributions to charity.

14.
    a. The game was lost by our team when the touchdown was scored by Jones.
    b. The game was lost by our team when Jones scored a touchdown.
    c. Our team lost the game when Jones scored a touchdown.
    d. Our team lost the game when a touchdown was scored by Jones.

15.
    a. Being as I am a student, I must buy many books.
    b. Since I am a student, I must buy many books.
    c. Being that I am a student, I must buy many books.
    d. Since I am a student, many books must be bought.

16.
    a. The window was busted.
    b. The window was broke.
    c. The window was broken.
    d. The window was breaked.

17.
    a. I like to lay out in the sun.
    b. I like to lie out in the sun.
    c. I like to laid out in the sun.
    d. I like laying out in the sun.

18.
    a. The pie consists of sugar, peanut butter, and egg.
    b. The pie consist of sugar, peanut butter, and egg.
    c. Sugar, peanut butter, and egg consisted the pie.
    d. The consistence of the pie were sugar, peanut butter, and egg.

19.
    a. The captain, along with the rest of the team, were tired.
    b. The captain, along with the rest of the team, was tired.
    c. The captain and the team was tired.
    d. The captain and the rest of the team was tired.

20.
    a. The jury gave their decision to the judge.
    b. The jury gave it's decision to the judge.
    c. The jury gave its decision to the judge.
    d. The jury gave there decision to the judge.

21.
    a. Last night the coach complained about the team play, but John says it plays well.
    b. Last night the coach complains about the team play, but John says it plays well.
    c. Last night the coach complained about the team play, but John said it plays well.
    d. Last night the coach complained about the team play, but John said it played well.

Directions: Each item below may contain an error in sentence construction—a fragment, a comma splice, or a fused (run-on) sentence. NO ITEM HAS MORE THAN ONE ERROR. Mark the letter which **precedes** the group of words containing the error. Mark **E** if there is no error.

22.
(a) John was now at the top of his class in physics. (b) John, who had done poorly in high school. (c) John had let his friends influence him, and he never found time to study. (d) He wanted to do well now because he wanted to show his parents and former teachers that their predictions for failure were wrong.

23.
(a) This was what he had waited for: a chance to prove to others that he knew better than they about his intelligence. (b) He invited his parents to the program, not telling them that he would receive an award; he also invited his former science teacher. (c) They all sat together jammed into the small physics lecture hall they waited patiently for the announcement of the awards for top students. (d) When John's name was called, his father laughed, thinking it was a joke, but his mother beamed with pride as John walked up to receive the award.

24.
(a) John's high school physics teacher could hardly believe that John had finally learned to study, he got a lump in his throat and a tear in his eye. (b) He heard Dr. Smith, the famous physicist, praise John; furthermore, he heard John say he planned to major in physics. (c) When John returned to his seat, his former teacher congratulated him and wished him well in his college work. (d) John told him that he appreciated all of his efforts to help him learn and said that his interest in physics began in that high school class.

Writing

The items below may contain errors in punctuation. NO ITEM HAS MORE THAN ONE ERROR. Mark the letter indicating the sentence which contains a punctuation error. Mark E if there is no error.

25.

(a) The record for the long jump was won by a young woman, who had not been particularly athletic before. (b) Mary Fenton, a lean, tall, twenty-three year old, had to take off her glasses before every jump. (c) She had an advantage over the other jumpers: without her glasses, she saw their marks in a blurred way and couldn't tell if she needed to beat a record. (d) As she heard the cheers of the crowd, she knew that she had won; she jumped up and reached for her glasses from her happy coach.

26.

(a) The storm blew in from the sea, and it swept over the tiny town with great sheets of rain. (b) On June 20, 1983 the houses on Mulberry Street lost their roofs and many also lost porches and garages. (c) Weather observers watched, their eyes straining to see if a funnel cloud would appear - the sign of sure destruction. (d) When the fury of the storm had passed, everyone felt lucky that no one had been killed.

27.

(a) The instructor urged the students to, "study every night, call if you have questions, and review for the tests." (b) He said that he was "always available"; however, when I phoned him, no one answered. (c) I felt bad when I found out that he had been in an accident, but he said, "Don't worry about me." (d) He helped me in class, on the phone, and at the review sessions.

28.

(a) The reporter took the following information: Jane Baird, president; John Larkin, vice-president; and Terry Martin, secretary. (b) All of the officers were happy that the press covered their first meeting; they had important business to discuss. (c) Their first order of business was to make an announcement, dues would increase by 50%. (d) The members were furious to hear the news.

Directions: The items below may contain errors in capitalization. NO ITEM HAS MORE THAN ONE ERROR. Mark the letter which locates the sentence containing an error in capitalization. Mark E if there is no error.

29.
   a. The church bulletin stated that the Youth Fellowship would meet on January 29, 1984.
   b. The meeting was set for 2:00 p.m. in the Forest Building on Main Street.
   c. Everyone was to bring something for the Paytons who were retiring in February.
   d. John and Mary brought some Nature's Wonder candy for the Paytons.

30.
   a. I tried to enjoy the holidays, but I kept thinking of Elizabeth who was still in Good Samaritan Hospital.
   b. She was in traction because of her broken leg, and her Mother said it would be three more weeks until she could leave the hospital.
   c. I had visited her often, but she had told me not to come on Christmas or New Year's.
   d. She said that she would have enough company with her cousins and the doctors and nurses, especially Dr. Maxwell, visiting her.

31.
   a. My grades in physics, algebra, and French were good.
   b. Psychology was another story; in Adolescent Psychology 201, I was afraid I would fail.
   c. My past semesters' grades would help however: my average was a 3.0 in other psychology classes.
   d. If only I could pass, I was sure that I could get into the Bellwood University graduate school.

32.
   a. I read **Requiem for a Heavyweight** last year.
   b. The best part was when Joe told his manager that he "was through with fighting forever."
   c. His manager said, " you don't know how long I've waited for you to make that decision."
   d. That last fight in Philadelphia had convinced Joe that he could get killed in the ring if he fought Rocky again.

Writing

Directions: The following sentences contain common spelling errors. Choose the correct alternative for each item.

33. I need some (a) comparative (b) comparitive data on those computers before I buy one.

34. He was a star (a) athelete (b) athlete in college.

35. She had a hard time finding (a) accomodations (b) accommodations at the popular vacation spot.

36. You will find the Happy Wanderer Inn a nice (a) enviroment (b) environment for a honeymoon.

Check your answers for Writing Test A below. If you made any errors, review the specific competency and instruction. Note the correct answer. Then take Writing Test B to see if you have improved your writing competencies.

Answers to Writing Test A
1. C	2. D	3. D	4. B	5. A	6. D	7. A	8. D	9. D	10. D
11. B	12. C	13. D	14. C	15. B	16. C	17. B	18. A	19. B	20. C
21. D	22. B	23. C	24. A	25. A	26. B	27. A	28. C	29. E	30. B
31. D	32. C	33. A	34. B	35. B	36. B				

WRITING TEST B

Multiple Choice: Select the best answer. Do not mark more than one answer.

Directions: Complete each sentence by choosing the most effective word or phrase which conforms to standard written English.

1. The clerk's attitude_____

        a. ticked me off.
        b. angered me.
        c. got me mad.
        d. caused me to feel anger.

2. Today Joe Smith was _____charged at the police station for the theft of the money.

        a. formally
        b. formal
        c. formerly
        d. form

3. The boss said that we had _____ to throw it away when the new paper comes.

        a. too much stationary
        b. to much stationary
        c. too much stationery
        d. to much stationery

4. The report was _____to understanding why they made those plans.

        a. quiet valuable
        b. quite valuable
        c. quiet invaluable
        d. quite invaluable

Writing

5. The _____ was interviewed by the school board.

    a. perspective principal
    b. perspective principle
    c. prospective principal
    d. prospective principle

6. Although he_____, he was able to go on the business trip.

    a. was sick as a dog
    b. became ill
    c. got sick
    d. felt indisposed

Directions: Choose the sentence that expresses the thought most clearly and effectively and that has no errors in structure.

7.
    a. Eating with their fingers, the chicken and french fries soon disappeared.
    b. Since they ate with their fingers, the chicken and french fries were consumed by them.
    c. Eating with their fingers, they soon ate all of the chicken and french fries.
    d. The chicken and french fries were eaten by them being that they used their fingers to eat.

8.
    a. When girl-watching, his car hit a tree.
    b. He was driving along girl-watching when his car collided with a tree.
    c. When he was driving, he was girl-watching and a tree was hit.
    d. When he was girl-watching, he drove his car into a tree.

9.
    a. Mr. Jones was lazy, dirty, and he drank all of the time.
    b. Mr. Jones, a lazy man, was dirty and liked to drink all of the time.
    c. Mr. Jones was lazy, dirty, and drinking all of the time.
    d. Mr. Jones was lazy, dirty, and drunken all of the time.

10.   a. Because she trained hard, she won the race.
         b. Because she trained hard is the reason she won the race.
         c. She trained hard, and she won the race.
         d. Training hard is what caused her to win the race.

11.   a. His motorcycle was hit by a car on the way to the store.
         b. On the way to the store, his motorcycle was hit by a car.
         c. His motorcycle was hit by a car when it was on the way to the store.
         d. When he was on his way to the store, his motorcycle was hit by a car.

12.   a. Prices have arisen more this year than ever.
         b. Prices have rose more this year than ever.
         c. Prices have risen more this year than ever.
         d. Prices have raised more this year than ever.

13.   a. The board of directors gave its decision Saturday.
         b. The board of directors gave their decision Saturday.
         c. The board of directors gave there decision Saturday.
         d. The board of directors gave it's decision Saturday.

14.   a. The general, as well as all of the surviving troops, were celebrating.
         b. The general, as well as all of the surviving troops, was celebrating.
         c. The general and the surviving troops was celebrating.
         d. The general and all of the surviving troops was celebrating.

15.   a. The boys knew that each of them were at fault.
         b. The boys knew that each of them was at fault.
         c. The boys knew that each of them is at fault.
         d. The boys knew that each of them are at fault.

16.   a. Many of the restless needs a plan for his life.
         b. Many of the restless need a plan for his life.
         c. Many of the restless needs a plan for their life.
         d. Many of the restless need a plan for their lives.

17.
    a. Mary and me are taller than him.
    b. Mary and I are taller than he.
    c. Mary and I are taller than him.
    d. Mary and me are taller than him.

18.
    a. If you will speak to whoever is in charge, you will get fast service.
    b. If you will speak to whomever is in charge, you will get fast service.
    c. If you will speak to who is in charge, you will get fast service.
    d. If you will speak to the person in charge, fast service will be given to you.

19.
    a. If your work is finished, you can lay down to rest.
    b. If your work is finished, you can lie down to rest.
    c. If your work is finished, you can be laying down to rest.
    d. If your work is finished, you can laid down to rest.

20.
    a. Bill goes in, sits down, and said that he was angry.
    b. Bill goes in, sat down, and said that he was angry.
    c. Bill goes in, sits down, and says that he is angry.
    d. Bill goes in, sits down, and says that he was angry.

21.
    a. The man whom I thought was the manager talked to us workers.
    b. The man whom I thought was the manager talked to we workers.
    c. The man who I thought was the manager talked to us workers.
    d. The man who I thought was the manager talked to we workers.

Directions: Each item below may contain an error in sentence construction—a fragment, a comma splice, or a fused (run-on) sentence. NO ITEM HAS MORE THAN ONE ERROR. Mark the letter which **precedes** the group of words containing the error. Mark **E** if there is no error.

22.
(a) Spring break gave me the opportunity to see some of my old friends. (b) After we had all studied hard during the winter and had taken our midterms. (c) We were in need of a change of pace. (d) We stayed up late, talked and laughed a great deal, and had a good time telling each other how hard our classes were.

23.   (a) John and Jim had gone away to college in Boston, so they had many stories to tell about big city activities. (b) They felt lonely at first, but they adjusted to the subways, night-life, and high prices. (c) I did not envy their experiences they had forgotten all of the simple pleasures of the beach and small town life. (d) After they left to go back to school, I thought a long time about how much they had changed.

24.   (a) I was happy to see some of my other friends, they didn't seem to have changed as much. (b) We had a great time at the beach and in the park where we used to play and relax when we were in high school. (c) After seeing John and Jim again, I knew that my decision to stay here to go to college had been the right one for me. (d) They were happy with their decision to go away because they wanted to live in a large city after graduation, but I want to stay near my family when I begin my career.

Directions: The items below may contain errors in punctuation.   NO ITEM HAS MORE THAN ONE ERROR. Mark the letter indicating the sentence which contains a punctuation error.   Mark E if there is no error.

25.   (a) My course in economics is difficult, and it keeps me studying every night. (b) I never thought much about why interest rates were high; now I know all of the influences on the rates. (c) Now I understand why bankers watch trends: they can predict increases and decreases in the prime interest rate. (d) My instructor is an excellent, well-organized person, who keeps up with current events better than anyone I know.

26.   (a) My instructor for my jogging class can outrun any of us, because he has been training for the marathon. (b) He tells us how to pace ourselves, how to extend our running each week, and how to keep track of our progress; he knows how to make us do our best. (c) If he keeps training with us in our class and also on his own, he may qualify to run in the marathon this year. (d) Even if he doesn't qualify, he will be in better shape than anyone I know, and I predict that he will have a great sense of well being.

Writing

27.   (a) My history instructor said, "Learn the basic concepts and historical patterns, and you won't need to memorize dates and battles." (b) She said that, "history is best understood when the student hangs the dates and places on the framework of the period and its patterns" rather than learning isolated bits of data. (c) After she told us how to study history, I began to study differently, and, consequently, I made better grades. (d) If only I had learned this valuable information earlier, I might have chosen history as my major because I have always been interested in it.

28.   (a) The following people made the President's List: Mary Turner, Clearwater, Janice Martin, Orlando, Joe Smith, Miami, Clark Kenner, Tallahassee, and Donald Hughes, Tampa. (b) They were notified by letter to come to the college Convocation to receive a certificate; all were present. (c) Their parents also attended, and they were very proud of their children's efforts. (d) I am going to try to achieve this honor next semester, but it won't be easy because of the kinds of classes I am taking.

Directions: The items below may contain errors in capitalization. NO ITEM HAS MORE THAN ONE ERROR. Mark the letter which locates the sentence containing an error in capitalization.   Mark E if there is no error.

29.   a. Joe Tanner who was president last year will be the featured speaker for this year's Florida Conference in Orlando.
       b. His topic will be "The Rise And Fall Of The Citrus Industry."
       c. Most of the growers, especially Mary and Jim Manning, will be eager to hear his speech in the Tangerine Ballroom.
       d. After his speech, Mr. Tanner will fly to Washington, D. C. to address a Senate subcommittee on farm interests.

30.   a. Next year I will be taking calculus, French, and physical education.
       b. My physical education class is PED 201 Weight Training, but I am hoping to take bowling after that.
       c. My calculus class is required for all business majors.
       d. My French class involves the study of French Literature.

31.
    a. When I graduate, I plan to drive to Miami for an interview at the Cooper Company.
    b. I hear that they are a great company to work for, and I want to try to begin my career with their president, Mr. Jack Gener.
    c. My past experience with public relations during summers will give me an edge toward getting a job in the newsroom in Fort Lauderdale.
    d. If I can't work there, maybe I will find something else to do in the southeast.

32.
    a. When I heard that recording of Mary Martin singing in "South Pacific," I could see why that musical remained so popular for years.
    b. The song "Some Enchanted Evening" is one of my all-time favorites, but John doesn't particularly like it.
    c. I hope to see the movie on channel 13 sometime in January, 1984.
    d. One of the dinner theaters will be doing a revival of "South Pacific" this spring, so I may get to see it then if I miss the movie.

Directions: The following sentences contain common spelling errors. Choose the correct alternative for each item.

33. I studied the effects of the Watergate scandal on the (a) goverment, (b) government.

34. The scandal (a) embarrassed, (b) embarassed many followers of Richard Nixon.

35. My philosophy class studies theories on the meaning of (a) existance, (b) existence.

36. That drug (a) affects (b) effects coordination and balance, so you should not take it.

Check your answers for Writing Test B below. If you made any errors, review the specific competency and instruction.

ANSWERS TO WRITING TEST B

1. B	2. A	3. C	4. B	5. C	6. B	7. C	8. D	9. D	10. A
11. D	12. C	13. A	14. B	15. B	16. D	17. B	18. A	19. B	20. C
21. C	22. B	23. C	24. A	25. D	26. A	27. B	28. A	29. B	30. D
31. D	32. C	33. B	34. A	35. B	36. A				

Contributed by

Palm Beach

Junior College

Contributed by Florida State University

MATHEMATICS

MATHEMATICS INTRODUCTION

The mathematics portion of the College Level Academic Skills Test includes items from arithmetic, algebra, logic, geometry, probability and statistics, and computers. Further, the student is tested with respect to algorithms, concepts, generalizations, and problem solving of all of the topics above except computers.

This chapter presents the fifty-six mathematics competencies that will be covered on CLAST examination. Short descriptions of the competencies are given in the context of two sample tests which have been designed to simulate the questions that will appear on the actual CLAST examination. Each of the mathematics competencies includes a number of sub-skills; therefore, each sample test is much longer than the mathematics portion of the actual CLAST examination.

Each CLAST objective may require four test questions to cover all possible methods of testing the objective. These two tests attempt to include all the ways to test each objective. Some of the ways to test an objective will be in test A and the rest in test B. The serious student will need to complete all the problems in both tests to cover CLAST thoroughly.

The actual CLAST examination contains fifty-six questions to be answered in 90 minutes. Each test usually contains extra questions that are being tested for use in subsequent exams and are not counted.

Detailed solutions for each sample test immediately follow the test. These solutions show how the correct answer is found and frequently explain why other possible answers are incorrect.

COLLEGE LEVEL SKILLS IN COMPUTATION

Students are expected to demonstrate mastery of the four basic operations of arithmetic (addition, subtraction, multiplication, and division) for whole numbers, fractions, and mixed numbers. You can expect some straight-forward computations like those illustrated in problems 1-4 below.

1. Add: $\frac{3}{4} + \frac{5}{6}$

    a. $\frac{8}{10}$　　b. $\frac{4}{5}$　　c. $1\frac{7}{12}$　　d. $\frac{8}{12}$　　e. $\frac{19}{24}$　　f. $\frac{7}{12}$

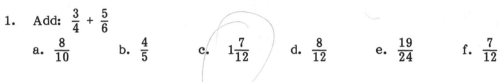

2. Subtract: $8\frac{7}{8} - 1\frac{1}{4}$

    a. $7\frac{5}{8}$　　b. $7\frac{3}{4}$　　c. $\frac{5}{8}$　　d. $7\frac{6}{4}$　　e. $7\frac{5}{4}$　　g. none are correct

3. Multiply: $\frac{3}{8} \times 1\frac{1}{3}$

    a. $\frac{1}{2}$　　b. $1\frac{1}{8}$　　c. 2　　d. $\frac{12}{112}$　　e. $\frac{3}{6}$　　f. $\frac{9}{32}$

4. Divide: $3\frac{1}{2} \div \frac{1}{2}$

    a. $1\frac{3}{4}$　　b. 7　　c. $\frac{1}{7}$　　d. $\frac{7}{4}$　　e. $\frac{7}{2}$　　f. $\frac{4}{7}$

Computations with decimal numerals will be tested with the expectation that students will demonstrate mastery of the four basic operations of arithmetic. Straightforward computations like those in problems 5-8 will be encountered.

5. Add: .595 + .63

    a. .1225   b. 1.225   c. .658   d. .0658   e. 1.125
    f. none are correct

6. Subtract: 310.5 - 2.025

    a. 1080   b. 1.08   c. 308.575   d. 308.475   e. 108.0
    f. none are correct

7. Multiply: 10.6 x .03

    a. 318   b. 31.8   c. .318   d. 3.18   e. .0318
    f. none are correct

8. Divide: $0.265 \div .05$

    a. .0053   b. 5.3   c. .53   d. 53   e. none are correct

> *Students are expected to correctly round off two types of numerals:*
>> *(1) Given a measurement, the student must demonstrate an ability to round the measurement off to a stated degree of accuracy.*
>> *(2) Given a decimal numeral, the student must demonstrate an ability to round the numeral off at a particular place value.*
>
> *Rounding off competencies are illustrated below by problems 9-11.*

9. Round off to the nearest centimeter (cm): 34.8 cm

    a. 34.9 cm   b. 35 cm   c. 34 cm   d. 3 cm

10. Round off to the nearest hundred pounds: 7425 pounds

    a. 7400   b. 7500   c. 7200   d. 7420   e. 7430

11. Round the measurement of segment AB to the nearest $\frac{1}{4}$ inch.

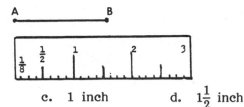

   a. $1\frac{1}{4}$ inch   b. $1\frac{3}{8}$ inch   c. 1 inch   d. $1\frac{1}{2}$ inch

The student is expected to demonstrate an ability to find the surface area of two-dimensional geometric figures and the volume of three-dimensional geometric figures. The types of figures that will be used and questions that can be asked are illustrated by problems 12-14 below.

12. Find the volume of a room 40 meters long, 25 meters wide, and 3 meters high.

   a. 3000 cu. m   b. 68 cu. m   c. 3000 m   d. 68 m
   e. none are correct

13. What is the surface area of a rectangular solid that is 8 inches by 2 inches by 10 inches?

   a. 160 square inches   b. 160 inches   c. 232 cubic inches
   d. 232 square inches

14. What is the circumference of a circle that has a diameter of 6 cm?

   a. 6π cm   b. 18π cm   c. 36π sq. cm   d. 9π sq. cm

Given a relationship between two quantities the student is expected to demonstrate the use of that relationship when given an actual number for one of the quantities. This skill is illustrated by the problem 15.

15. What is the volume in cubic centimeters of a flask that will hold 1.75 liters?

   a. 1.75 cu. cm   b. 17.5 cu. cm   c. 175 cu. cm   d. 1750 cu. cm

The student is expected to demonstrate an ability to add, subtract, multiply, and divide real number expressions. Problems 16-19 below illustrate the type of expressions that may be on the test for this competency.

16. Add: $-3\pi + -7\pi - 5 =$

    a. -15π b. $10\pi - 5$ c. $-10\pi - 5$ d. -5π

    e. $-10 - 5\pi$ f. 5π

17. Multiply: $\sqrt{3} \times \sqrt{6}$

    a. $3\sqrt{2}$ b. $\sqrt{18}$ c. 18 d. 3 e. 324

18. Subtract: $\sqrt{50} - \sqrt{18}$

    a. $2\sqrt{2}$ b. $\sqrt{32}$ c. $4\sqrt{2}$ d. $-2\sqrt{2}$ e. $3\sqrt{3}$

19. Divide: $15 \div 3\sqrt{2}$

    a. $\dfrac{5}{\sqrt{2}}$ b. $\dfrac{5\sqrt{2}}{2}$ c. $\dfrac{5\sqrt{2}}{4}$ d. $\dfrac{\sqrt{2}}{5}$ e. $45\sqrt{30}$

    f. $5\sqrt{\dfrac{15}{2}}$

Skills of elementary algebra are a major part of the competencies expected of every Florida Sophomore. One type of algebraic skill requires the student to demonstrate an ability to simplify numerical and simple algebraic expressions. Problems 20-22 illustrate this competency.

20. Simplify: $2 \times 3 + 8 \div 2$

    a. 7 b. 10 c. 14 d. $7\frac{1}{2}$ e. 11

21. Simplify: $-14t - 2t \times 3 + 21t^2 \div 7 \times 3$

    a. $9t^2 - 20t$ b. $-20t + t^2$ c. $9t^2$ d. $-48t + t^2$

22. Simplify: 6t − (5t) x (2) + 3t
    a. 5t   b. −t   c. t   d. 7t   e. −19t

Students are expected to demonstrate an ability to compute using scientific notation numerals. This skill includes the ability to read and write decimal numerals using scientific notation. Problems 23-24 illustrate the type of problem that may be used to test your ability to handle scientific notation numerals. A selection from the four operations of addition, subtraction, multiplication or division may be expected.

23. Use scientific notation to find the answer: $\dfrac{2.4 \times 10^3}{1.2 \times 10^{-2}}$

    a. 2×10^5 b. 2×10^1 c. 2×10^{-5} d. $.2 \times 10^1$
    e. 3.6×10^1 f. 3.6×10^{-5}

24. Compute and give the answer in scientific notation. (.0004) x (170,000)
    a. 6.8×10^1 b. 6.8×10^2 c. 6.8×10^0 d. 6.8×10^9 e. 68

Another type of algebra skill expected of every Florida Sophomore is the ability to solve equations and inequalities. This competency is illustrated by problems 25-28 below.

25. If $3x - 1 \geq 5x + 5$, then:
    a. $x \geq -3$ b. $x \geq -2$ c. $x \leq -3$ d. $x \leq -2$ e. $x \geq \frac{1}{2}$

26. If $5x - 2 = 3x + 6$, then:
    a. 4   b. 2   c. $\frac{1}{2}$ d. 1   e. $\frac{1}{4}$

27. If $\frac{2}{3}x = 15$, then

    a. 10   b. $14\frac{1}{3}$ c. $\frac{30}{3}$ d. $22\frac{1}{2}$

28. If $3(x + 2) = 2[x - (1 - x)]$, then:

    a. 8   b. -1   c. $-\frac{8}{3}$ d. 1   e. none are correct

Formulas and equalities express relationships between quantities. Each student is expected to demonstrate an ability to correctly use formulas and other equalities. Problems 29-33 illustrate the level of skill expected.

29. Use the relation $y = x^2 + 2x - 3$ to find y when x = 0.

    a. 0   b. -3   c. 3   d. 6   e. none are correct

30. Use the relation $a = (b - 2)^2$ to find a when b = -1.

    a. 1   b. 5   c. 9   d. -3   e. none are correct

31. The formula for converting a Fahrenheit temperature to Celcius is $C = \frac{5}{9}(F - 32)$. What is the temperature on the Celcius scale when the Fahrenheit temperature is 86°?

    a. 15.75°   b. 30°   c. 115.5°   d. none are correct

32. The formula for converting a Celcius temperature to Fahrenheit is $F = \frac{9}{5}C + 32$. What is the Fahrenheit temperature when the Celcius temperature is 35°?

    a. 117°   b. 31°   c. 95°   d. none are correct

33. The formula for finding the simple interest(I) on a loan is I = PRT. How much interest will be charged on a car loan of $6,000 (P) at a 14% simple interest rate (R) for two years (T)?

    a. $168   b. $1,680.00   c. $16,800   d. $168,000
    e. none are correct

The ability of read and interpret data shown in bar graphs, line graphs, or circle graphs is expected of sophomores. Samples of the type graph that may be encountered are found in Problems 34-36.

34. The graph on the right represents the monthly sales of the Mace Plumbing Company. How much higher are the sales in October than in January?

    a. $4,000   b. $40,000
    c. $20,000   d. $2,000
    e. $60,000   f. $6,000

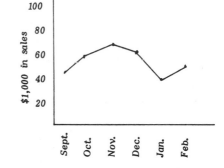

35. The graph shows the average temperature at 2 PM for the days shown. Find the average temperature on Thursday.

    a. 40°
    b. 52°
    c. 62°
    d. 65°
    e. 57°

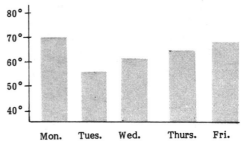

Average Daily Temperatures

36. The number of hours required in each discipline of a college core curriculum is represented in the circle graph at the right. What percent of these hours is in English and natural science combined?

    a. 18.94%   d. 74.2%
    b. 47.2%   e. 52.7%
    c. 25%   f. 27.6%

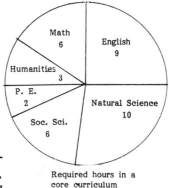

Required hours in a core curriculum

Statistics is used to analyze data and predict future events based on the analysis. The statistical notions of mean, mode, and median are the competencies tested in Problems 37-39.

37. Find the <u>mean</u> of the numbers 5, 6, 5, 3, 6, 7, 6, 2.

    a. 6   b. 5   c. 5.5   d. 4   e. none are correct

38. Find the <u>median</u> of the numbers 3,5,5,6,8,6,12,9,6,10.

    a. 6   b. 7   c. 6.5   d. 8   e. none are correct

39. Find the <u>mode</u> of the numbers 21,30,32,21,25,21,21,23,22

    a. 21   b. 22   c. 24   d. 22.5   e. 21.5

A knowledge of probability is expected of Florida Sophomores. The competency of identifying a random event is illustrated in Problem 40.

40. A blue box contains two cards labeled 5 and 9. A red box contains two cards labeled 2 and 6. Two cards are randomly selected, the first from the blue box and the second from the red box. Which set represents an appropriate sample space for this experiment?

    a. $\{(5,9),(9,5),(2,6),(6,2)\}$ b. $\{(5,2),(5,6),(9,2),(9,6)\}$

    c. $\{(2,5),(2,9),(6,5),(6,9)\}$ d. $\{(5,6),(5,2),(6,5),(6,9)\}$

    e. none are correct

Venn diagrams are useful for demonstrating relationships between sets. The ability to identify the inclusion or exclusion of elements in a set is the competency required to complete Problems 41-42.

41. Sets A, B, C, and U are related as shown in the diagram.
Select the answer.
    1. An element which is a member of set B is also a member of U.
    2. An element which is a member of set A and set B is not a member of set C.
    3. An element which is a member of U is also a member of B.

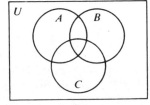

    a. 1 only   b. 2 only   c. 3 only   d. 1 and 2 only

    e. 2 and 3 only   f. 1 and 3 only   g. all are true

42. Sets A, B, C and U are related as shown in the diagram. Select the answer.
    1. An element which is a member of set A and set C is also a member of set C.
    2. An element is a member of A only if it is a member of U.
    3. An element is a member of U only if it is a member of C.

   a. 1 only
   b. 2 only
   c. 3 only
   d. 1 and 2 only
   e. 1 and 3
   f. 2 and 3
   g. all are correct

Exponents are useful in many ways. A test item for this competency is shown by problem 43.

43. Select the equivalent expression for $(2^3)(5^2)$.
   a. $2 + 2 + 2 + 5 + 5$
   b. 10^6
   c. 10^5
   d. $2(2)(2)(5)(5)$
   e. $(2 + 5)^5$
   f. $(2 + 5)^{10}$
   g. 6×10

Students are expected to demonstrate mastery of the concepts of place value in base-ten and other numeration systems. This competency is demonstrated in Problems 44-45.

44. Select the place value associated with the underlined digit. 36.0$\underline{5}$6
   a. $\frac{1}{10}$
   b. $\frac{1}{10^2}$
   c. $\frac{1}{10^3}$
   d. $\frac{1}{10^0}$
   e. none are correct

45. Find the base-ten equivalent to 224 (base-five.)
   a. 24
   b. 54
   c. 44
   d. 64
   e. none are correct

Numbers can be expressed as decimals, percents or fractions. The ability to identify equivalent forms of such numerals is a Florida competency. Problems 46-48 are examples of the type problems that can be expected.

46. Identify the equivalent expression to 0.2.
   a. .2%
   b. 2%
   c. 20%
   d. 0.2%
   e. .02%

47. Identify the equivalent expression to 150%.

    a. .015   b. $\frac{150}{100}$%   c. 1.5   d. 15.0   e. 150

48. Identify the equivalent expression to $\frac{13}{25}$.

    a. 52   b. .052   c. .52%   d. 52%   e. .052%

Another competency related to decimals, fractions, and percents is the ability to identify the larger or smaller number when given a pair of the numbers. Some of the pairs of numbers that can be expected are shown in Problems 49-53.

49. Choose the symbol for $\frac{3}{4}$ [ ] $\frac{8}{9}$.

    a. <   b. >   c. =

50. Choose the symbol for $\frac{2}{3}$ [ ] $-\frac{8}{9}$.

    a. <   b. >   c. =

51. Choose the symbol for $1.2\overline{5}$ [ ] $1.\overline{25}$

    a. <   b. >   c. =

52. Choose the symbol for .30 [ ] $\frac{1}{5}$

    a. <   b. >   c. =

53. Choose the symbol for 6.32 [ ] 6.032

    a. <   b. >   c. =

Students are expected to recognize certain relationships between lines as part of their knowledge of geometry. An illustration of the type figure that will be tested is shown in Problem 54.

54. The diagram on the right shows lines in the same plane. Line m_4 is vertical. Select the answer.
    1. Lines m_1 and m_4 are neither parallel nor intersecting.
    2. Lines m_3 and m_4 are intersecting but not perpendicular.
    3. Lines m_2 and m_1 are both parallel and horizontal.

    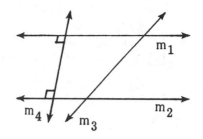

    a. 1 only   b. 2 only   c. 3 only   d. 1 and 2 only
    e. 1 and 3 only   f. 2 and 3 only   g. none are correct

Another geometric concept tested will be the knowledge of angle relationships when given triangles or parallel lines. Problems 55-56 are examples of the level of knowledge expected.

55. For the figure at the right, which statement/s is/are true? The notation $m \angle Z = 30°$ means the measure of angle Z is 30°.
    1. AC is perpendicular to BC.
    2. $m \angle 1 = m \angle 4 + m \angle 3$
    3. $m \angle 2 + m \angle 3 = 90°$
    4. $\angle 1$ and $\angle 2$ are supplementary.

    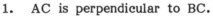

    a. 1 only   b. 2 only   c. 3 only   d. 4 only   e. 1,2,3 only
    f. 2,3,4 only   g. 1,3,4 only   h. 2 and 3 only   i. 3 and 4 only

56. For the figure on the right, which statement is true? Line m_1 is parallel to line m_2

    1. Since $m \angle 4 = 41°$, $m \angle 3 = 65°$
    2. Since $m \angle 5 = m \angle 1$, $m \angle 6 = m \angle 2$
    3. $\angle 1$ and $\angle 3$ are complementary.

    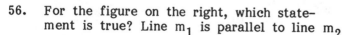

    a. 1 only   b. 2 only   c. 3 only   d. 1 and 2   e. 1 and 3
    f. 2 and 3   g. none are correct

The knowledge of properties of some basic geometric figures is to be demonstrated by Florida Sophomores. The kind of figures that will be used are shown in Problems 57-60.

57. Select the geometric figure that possesses **all** of the following characteristics.

    1. quadrilateral   2. diagonals are congruent
    3. opposite sides are parallel

    a. rhombus   b. parallelogram   c. trapezoid   d. rectangle
    e. none are correct

58. The words "right," "acute," "obtuse," "scalene," "isosceles," and "equilateral" are used individually to describe triangles. Which of the following word descriptions is/are incorrect because it/they impose/s impossible conditions on a triangle.
    1. Right, isosceles   3. Right, obtuse
    2. Isosceles, acute   4. Right, equilateral
    a. 1 only   b. 2 only   c. 3 only   d. 4 only   e. 1 and 2 only
    f. 2 and 3 only   g. 3 and 4 only   h. 2 and 4 only

59. Which of the following is an acute angle?
    a.   b.   c.   d.

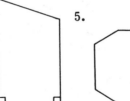

60. Which of the following figures is/are rectangles?
    1.   2.   3.   4.   5.

    a. 1 only   b. 2 only   c. 3 only   d. 4 only   e. 5 only
    f. 1 and 2 only   g. 3 and 4 only   h. 2 and 4 only   i. 4 and 5 only

The ability to identify similar triangles and recognize the accompanying proportions is expected of students in Florida. The style of question that will be asked is demonstrated in Problems 61-63.

61. For the triangles on the right which of the following are true?

    1. $\angle X \cong \angle Y$ 4. $\dfrac{BC}{BA} = \dfrac{BD}{BE}$

    2. $\angle Y \cong \angle Z$

    3. $\dfrac{6}{8} = \dfrac{BE}{BC}$

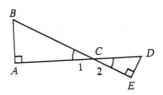

    a. 1 only   b. 2 only   c. 3 only   d. 1 and 2 only
    e. 3 and 4 only f. 2 and 3 only g. 1 and 4 only

62. Which of the sets of pictured triangles contain(s) similar triangles?
    1.   2.   3.

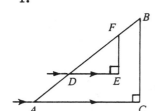
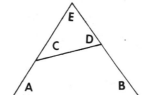

    a. 1 only   b. 2 only   c. 3 only   d. 1 and 2 only
    e. 1 and 3 only   f. 2 and 3   g. all are correct

63. Which statement/s 1, 2, or 3 is/are true for the pictured triangles? The notation $m(\overline{AB})$ denotes the measure or length of $\overline{AB}$ and not the segment AB itself.

    Note: The symbol $\lambdabar$ denotes that the angles are equal.

    1. $\dfrac{DE}{AB} = \dfrac{EC}{CA}$

    2. $m(\overline{DE}) = 3$

    3. $\angle W \cong \angle Z$

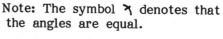
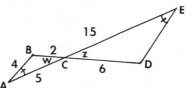

    a. 1 only   b. 2 only   c. 3 only   d. 1 and 2 only
    e. 1 and 3 only f. 2 and 3 only g. 1,2,3

Measurement of geometric objects is a skill expected of Florida students. Three types of measure will be tested. Problems 64-66 demonstrate the type items that may be used.

64. Identify the type of measure needed for segment $\overline{DB}$ in the figure shown.

    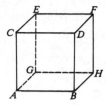

    a. linear   b. square
    c. cubic   d. surface
    e. metric

65. Identify the type of measure needed for the region with vertices ABCD of the figure in problem 64.

    a. linear   b. square   c. cubic   d. surface   e. metric

66. Identify the type of measure needed for the interior of the cylinder.

    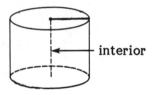

    a. linear
    b. square
    c. cubic
    d. surface
    e. metric

Students are expected to demonstrate a knowledge and use of algebraic operations and their properties. The level of skill and knowledge required is shown by Problems 67-70.

67. Identify the property of operation which is illustrated below:
    $(2 + 3x) + 5x = 2 + (3x + 5x)$

    a. Associative property of multiplication
    b. Associative property of addition
    c. Commutative property of addition
    d. Commutative property of multiplication
    e. Distributive property of multiplication over addition
    f. Identity property of multiplication
    g. Inverse property of multiplication

68. Identify the Property of operation which is illustrated below:
    $3(a) + 3(b) = 3(a + b)$

    a. Associative property of multiplication
    b. Associative property of addition
    c. Commutative property of addition
    d. Commutative property of multiplication
    e. Distributive property of multiplication over addition
    f. Identity property of multiplication
    g. Inverse property of multiplication

69. Which statement illustrates the commutative property of multiplication?

    a. $(a + b)(3) = a(3) + b(3)$ d. $-a + a = 0$

    b. $(a)(b) + c = (b)(a) + c$ e. $b \times (\frac{1}{b}) = 1$ if $b \neq 0$

    c. $a + b = b + a$ f. $a(b \times c) = (a \times b)c$

70. Choose the equivalent expression for: $5(7) + 5(a)$.

    a. $(5 \times 7)a$ b. $(5 + 7) + a$ c. $12(a)$ d. $35(a)$
    e. $5(7 + a)$ f. $5(12)(a)$ g. $(35 + 7)(a)$

    The ability to determine whether a number is
    a solution for an equation or inequality is
    important for an understanding of algebra.
    Examples of items that test for such know-
    ledge are shown by Problems 71-72.

71. Determine which of the following equations or inequalities have (–3) as a solution.
    1. $|x - 1| = 4$ 2. $(x + 4)(x + 2) \leq -1$ 3. $6x \leq x + 3$

    Which option below identifies every statement that has (–3) as a solution.

    a. 1 only   b. 2 only   c. 3 only   d. 1 and 2 only
    e. 1 and 3 only   f. 2 and 3 only   g. All are correct

72. Determine which of the following equations or inequalities have (–1) as a solution?

    1. $\frac{-1}{3} x = \frac{1}{3}$ 2. $(3x + 1)(x - 1) < 0$ 3. $-\frac{3}{5}x = -\frac{3}{5}$

    Which option below identifies every statement that has (–1) as a solution?

    a. 1 only   b. 2 only   c. 3 only   d. 1 and 2 only
    e. 1 and 3 only   f. 2 and 3 only   g. none are correct

*Other algebraic concepts to be demonstrat-
ed by Florida students are the ability to
recognize statements and conditions of proportion and variation. Problems 73-74
concern these topics.*

73. An average of 3 students make A's on math tests out of 8 students. If
x represents the number of students that make A's out of 450 students
select the equation that shows a correct proportion?

a. $\frac{3}{8} = \frac{450}{x}$ b. $\frac{3}{11} = \frac{x}{450}$ c. $\frac{3}{8} = \frac{x}{450}$ d. $\frac{3}{5} = \frac{450}{x}$

74. The distance an object travels is held constant while the rate of speed
and time vary. If the rate is 1,200 miles per hour when the time is 6
hours, select the statement of condition when the time is 4 hours and x
represents the rate?

a. $\frac{1200}{6} = \frac{x}{4}$ b. $\frac{x}{6} = \frac{4}{1200}$ c. $\frac{6}{1200} = \frac{4}{x}$ d. $\frac{1200}{x} = \frac{4}{6}$

*Graphing is an algebraic skill to be shown
by the sophomores. The test problems will
ask that students identify the graph associated with an inequality. Examples of inequalities that may be expected are found in
Problems 75-77.*

75. Which shaded region identifies the portion of the plane in which x ≥ 0,
y ≥ 0 and y ≤ 2?

a.   b.   c.   d.

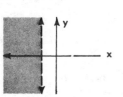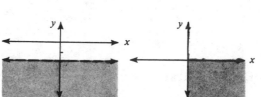

76. Which option gives the conditions
    that correspond to the shaded region
    of the plane shown at the right?

    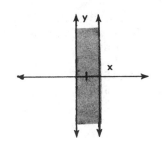

    a. $y \geq 0$ and $y \leq 2$
    b. $x \geq 0$ and $x = 2$
    c. $x \geq 0$ and $x \leq 2$
    d. $x \geq 0$ or $x \leq 2$

77. Which figure is the graph of $|x| + |y| = 2$.

    a.   b.   c.   d.

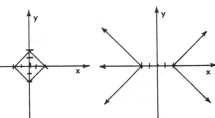

The normal curve is a statistical concept of
great importance. The ability to identify
the curve and its properties is to be demonstrated. The level of knowledge required
is shown by Problem 78.

78. Which of the following statements is/are true for a set of scores that
    are normally distributed?
    1. The probability that a score will fall between the mean and 1 stand-
        ard deviation above the mean is about 34%.
    2. The probability that a score is below 2 standard deviations below
        the mean is equal to the probability that a score is higher than 2
        standard deviations above the mean.
    3. About 50% of the scores are more than 2 standard deviations from
        the mean.
    4. The median of the scores is different from the mode.

    a. 1 only   b. 2 only   c. 3 and 4   d. 1 and 2   e. 1 and 4 only
    f. all are correct   g. none are correct

The concept of a sample is an important idea
in statistics. Students will be expected to
identify samples that are representative of
a population. Problem 79 illustrates the
type test item that may be used.

93

79. If the vehicles in a city are 40% large cars, 30% compact, and 30% trucks, which of the following samples is most representative of the vehicle population?

	large	compact	trucks	total
a.	425	425	350	1200
b.	250	200	200	650
c.	830	975	975	2780
d.	350	360	420	1130

e. none are correct

Another probability concept to be required is the ability to identify the probability that a certain event will occur in an experiment. The style of questions that may be asked is shown by Problems 80-81.

80. A box contains 3 red balls, 2 black balls, and 4 green balls. Two balls are drawn at random without replacement. Which expression shows the condition of the probability that both balls are red?

a. $\frac{3}{9} \times \frac{3}{9}$ b. $\frac{3}{9} \times \frac{2}{9}$ c. $\frac{3}{12} \times \frac{2}{11}$ d. $\frac{3}{9} + \frac{2}{8}$ e. $\frac{3}{9} \times \frac{2}{8}$

81. A coin is tossed two times. What is the probability of obtaining two heads or one head and one tail?

a. 1 b. $\frac{3}{4}$ c. $\frac{1}{2}$ d. $\frac{1}{4}$ e. 0

f. none are correct.

The ability to identify simple and compound statements and their negations is a skill in logic expected of sophomores. Examples of these test items are found in Problems 82-83.

82. Select the correct negation of the statement: "Sam is a barber and George is a butcher."

a. Sam is not a barber and George is not a butcher.
b. Sam is not a barber or George is not a butcher.
c. Sam is not a barber or George is a butcher.
d. Sam is a barber and George is not a butcher.
e. none are correct.

83. Select the statement that negates: "Bob wants to both go to the beach and go to a movie."

    a. Bob does not want to go to the beach and he does not want to go to a movie.

    b. If Bob wants to go to the beach, then he does not want to go to a movie.

    c. Bob does not want to go to the beach or he wants to go to the movie.

    d. Bob wants to go to the beach and he does not want to go to a movie.

Another skill in logic to be demonstrated by Florida students is the ability to determine whether two statements are equivalent. Problems 84-86 illustrate this type item.

84. Select the statement below which is **not** logically equivalent to "It is not true that both John and Jean are students."

    a. John is not a student and Jean is not a student.

    b. John is not a student or Jean is not a student.

    c. If John is a student, then Jean is not a student.

    d. If Jean is a student, then John is not a student.

85. Select the statement that is logically equivalent to: "If a fruit is a banana then it is yellow."

    a. If a fruit is not a banana then it is not yellow.

    b. If a fruit is yellow then it is not a banana.

    c. If a fruit is not yellow then it is not a banana.

    d. A fruit is a banana if it is yellow.

86. Select the negation of the statement "All geometric figures are rectangles."

    a. There are some geometric figures that are not rectangles.

    b. There are no rectangles that are geometric figures.

    c. There are no rectangles that are not geometric figures.

    d. There are no geometric figures that are not rectangles.

    e. There are some geometric figures that are rectangles.

In logic, a sentence that is an implication has three other forms, the converse, the inverse, and the contrapositive. Students will be expected to recognize these forms. Problem 87 illustrates such a question.

87. Select the converse of the statement "If Sally goes to school, Richard stays home."

    a. If Richard does not stay home, Sally does not go to school.
    b. If Sally does not go to school, Richard does not stay home.
    c. If Richard does not stay at home, Sally goes to school.
    d. If Richard stays home, Sally goes to school.

An important skill in logic is the ability to make logical conclusions when given a set of facts. The level of skill to be demonstrated is found in Problems 88-89.

88. Read the requirements and each applicant's application for obtaining a scholarship. Then identify the applicant that qualifies for the scholarship.

    To qualify for a scholarship, an athlete must have at least an "A" average in his/her senior year, place first or second in one event at the state level, and be less than 19 years old.

    <u>George</u> is 18 years 6 months old, had a "D" average in the senior year and won the mile race in the state meet.

    <u>Sara</u> is age 17, placed second in the 880 yard run at the state level and has a "B" average as a senior.

    <u>Selena</u> is 18 years old with a C average in her senior year. She placed <u>first</u> in the mile run in the regional meet.

    <u>Sam</u> placed first in the one and two mile events at the state meet. He is 20 years old and made an "A" average in his senior year.

    a. George   b. Sara   c. Selena   d. Sam   e. none are correct

89. Given that: All dogs are four-footed and
                      all terriers are dogs.
Determine which conclusions can be logically deduced.

    a. All dogs are terriers.
    b. No four-footed animals are terriers.
    c. All terriers are four-footed.
    d. Some terriers are four-footed.
    e. No terriers are four-footed.

Many arguments may have true conclusions but the arguments themselves are not logical. The ability to identify such arguments is a required competency and shown in Problem 90.

90. All of the following arguments have true conclusions, but not all of the arguments are valid. Select the argument(s) that are **not** valid.
    1. All fish can swim and all minnows are fish. Therefore all minnows can swim.
    2. All flies can wiggle and all insects can wiggle. As a result, all flies are insects.
    3. All babies have hair because all humans have hair and all babies are human.
    4. No educated people are dumb. Professors are not dumb. Therefore professors are educated people.

The ability to identify fallacious (invalid) arguments is a concept that is required knowledge of Florida students. There are several types of fallacious arguments as shown in Problems 91-93.

91. Which of the following arguments is/are fallacious?
    1. Sam cannot be trusted as Sam is a craftsman and crafty people can not be trusted.
    2. If Coover is elected everyone will have plenty to eat. Coover got elected, therefore Bill will not starve.
    3. Dr. Good, the family physician, says that a new law on abortion should not be passed. Therefore it should not be passed.

    a. 1 and 2 only   b. 1 and 3 only   c. 2 and 3 only   d. 1 only
    e. 2 only   f. 3 only   g. all are correct

92. Which of the following arguments is/are fallacious?
    1. All birds have feathers and Bill's parrot has feathers. Therefore it must be a bird.
    2. If a figure is a square then it is a rectangle and Mary's living room is a rectangle. Therefore it is a square.
    3. Marilyn can not buy at a wholesale appliance warehouse because she is a member of the same club as Janie and Janie is not allowed to buy at the warehouse.

    a. 1 only   b. 2 only   c. 3 only   d. 1 and 2 only
    e. 1 and 3 only   f. 2 and 3 only   g. all are fallacious

97

93. Which of the following arguments is/are **not** fallacious?
    1. If Mary is the prettiest girl at the dance she will have a good time and she is not the prettiest girl at the dance. As a result, she will not have a good time.
    2. Each element in the set of rational numbers has an inverse and the integers are part of the rational numbers. Therefore each integer has an inverse.
    3. Molly used to go to church because she replied "yes" when asked if she had stopped going to church.

    a. 1 only   b. 2 only   c. 3 only   d. none are fallacious

Another concept in logic important in mathematics is the idea of a proof by contradiction. Students will be expected to recognize when an argument is a proof by contradiction. Problem 94 shows the style of the test items that may be used.

94. Which of the following valid arguments illustrates a **proof by contradiction**?
    1. Mary is wet because if John pours water on Mary, then she will be wet and John did pour water on Mary.
    2. Juba could not buy hardware because he had $100 when he left home and he had to buy groceries for $60, gasoline for $20, lumber for $15, and hardware for $50. He came home with the needed groceries, gasoline, and lumber and 95 + 50 > 100.
    3. Dave went to the bank because he had to go to the bank and to the grocery.
    4. If Willie makes $100, then Sam will make $300 because if Willie makes $100 then Pearl will get a job and if Pearl gets a job, Sam will make $300.

Computers are rapidly making inroads into society. Florida students will be expected to demonstrate knowledge of the uses and abuses that can be made of computers. Problems 95-98 deal with these questions.

95. In a factory, a computer robot senses the correct spots to weld a car's roof to the body and makes the welds 24 hours a day.

    In the situation above, the computer's capabilities are suited to these tasks because they call for:

    a. speed   b. repetition   c. simulation   d. program modification

96. Efforts are being made to build fifth generation computers that will have human-like decision making abilities. Which situation below would require such capabilities.
    a. Perform the accounting tasks needed in a business.
    b. Make the decisions necessary to run a farm successfully all year long on the basis of data received during the year.
    c. Control the robots on an assembly line for washing machines.
    d. Interpret the data on a moon landing.

97. To use a computer to handle the accounting needs of a firm, Bob used a program which required that he gather the data and enter it in the computer. Then he followed the program instructions to get the computer to produce the balance sheets, income statements, and all the other needed accounting reports.
    To use the computer for this task which human function did Bob have to perform?

    a. make calculations.
    b. program the computer
    c. prepare and input the data
    d. modify the existing program

98. One abuse of computer use is that of obtaining information illegally. Which of the following situations illustrates this abuse?
    a. A computer "hacker" accesses the student information file of a college.
    b. The data generated by a computer was falsely assumed to be correct.
    c. A computer operator entered incorrect data on a system.
    d. A computer operator changes the names of the files in a system to divert money into her account from another randomly chosen account.

> *Florida Sophomores are expected to be able to generalize their knowledge in several areas. One of the areas is in numbers. The type of problem that will be tested is shown in Problems 99-100.*

99. Look for a common linear relationship between the numbers in each pair. Then find the missing term in the last pair.

    $(6,2)$, $(.3,.1)$, $(\frac{1}{2},\frac{1}{6})$, $(99,33)$, $(\frac{1}{3},\_)$

    a. $\frac{1}{2}$ b. $\frac{2}{3}$ c. $\frac{1}{3}$ d. $\frac{1}{9}$

100. Identify the missing term in the following geometric progression.

$$6, \ -3, \ \frac{3}{2}, \ -\frac{3}{4}, \ \frac{3}{8}, \ \underline{\hspace{1cm}}$$

a. $\frac{3}{16}$ b. $-\frac{3}{16}$ c. $-\frac{3}{6}$ d. $\frac{3}{6}$

Problems 101 and 102 illustrate the type objective covering the ability to generalize in the area of arithmetic.

101. Select the property or properties of operation(s) that could be used to simplify the given numerical expression in the least number of steps.

$$.54(1.01) + .54(2.1) = ?$$

a. Commutative property of addition and the distributive property
b. Associative property of multiplication
c. Distributive property of multiplication over addition
d. Distributive property and associative property of multiplication

102. Select the property or properties of operation(s) illustrated by this equation.

$$8(2 + 11) = 2 \times 8 + 8 \times 11$$

a. Commutative property of multiplication and the distributive property
b. Associative property of multiplication
c. Distributive property of multiplication over addition
d. Distributive property and associative property of multiplication

Florida Sophomores are expected to be able to generalize in the area of computing measures of geometric figure of 2 or 3 dimensions. Problems 103-104 illustrate this competency.

103. Study the figure on the right and select the formula for computing the total area of the pentagon.

a. area $= \frac{5}{2}bh$

b. area $= 5bh$

c. area $= 5(b + h)$

d. area $= \frac{5}{2}(b + h)$

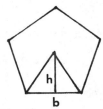

104. Select the formulas needed to calculate the total surface area of a cube topped by a square pyramid. Study the figures that make up the solid figure at the bottom.

a. surface area = $6s^2$

b. surface area = $5s^2 + 2sh$

c. surface area = $s^3 + \frac{1}{3}s^2h$

d. surface area = $5s^2 + 4sh$

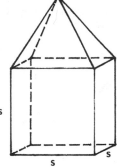

Face of
Pyramid

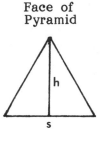

The ability to infer correct formulas to calculate measures of geometric figures is tested by problem 105. This item is a CLAST objective.

105. Study the figures on the right and select the correct formula for the measure (m) of an angle of a regular n-sided polygon.

a. $m = \dfrac{n(180)}{n-2}$

b. $m = \dfrac{n(180)}{n}$

c. $m = \dfrac{(n-2)(180)}{n}$

d. $m = \dfrac{(n-1)(180)}{n}$

3/sides: $m = \dfrac{180}{3} = 60°$

4/sides: $m = \dfrac{2(180)}{4} = 90°$

5/sides: $m = \dfrac{3(180)}{5} = 108°$

Florida sophomores will be required to demonstrate the ability to generalize in algebra with respect to inferring simple relations between variables. Problems 106 and 107 illustrate this objective.

Mathematics Test A

106. Study the examples:

$$a^3 * a^2 = a^7 \qquad a^2 * a^3 = a^8 \qquad a^5 * a^3 = a^{11}$$

Select the formula implied by the examples.

a. $a^x * a^y = a^{2x+y}$

b. $a^x * a^y = a^{xy}$

c. $a^x * a^y = a^{x+2y}$

d. $a^x * a^y = a^{xy+2}$

107. Study the examples:

$$x^4 \, \& \, x^6 \, \dagger \, x^2 = x^5 \qquad x^2 \, \& \, x^5 \, \dagger \, x^7 = x^1 \qquad x^5 \, \& \, x^3 \, \dagger \, x^4 = x^2$$

Select the formula implied by the examples.

a. $x^a \, \& \, x^b \, \dagger \, x^c = x^{\frac{a+b}{2}}$

b. $x^a \, \& \, x^b \, \dagger \, x^c = x^{\frac{a+b}{c}}$

c. $x^a \, \& \, x^b \, \dagger \, x^c = x^{\frac{ab}{2}}$

d. $x^a \, \& \, x^b \, \dagger \, x^c = x^{\frac{c+b}{a}}$

Problems 108 and 109 illustrate the competency of generalizing and selecting applicable properties for solving equations and inequalities

108. Select the property used to justify the following statement:
If $5 < x + 2 < 14$, then $3 < x < 12$

a. If $a + c > b + c$, then $a > b$.
b. If $a > b$ and $b > c$, then $a > c$.
c. If $ac > bc$ and $c > 0$, then $a > b$.
d. If $ac > bc$ and $c < 0$, then $a < b$.

109. Select the property used to justify the following statement:

If $-4x > 9$, then $x < -\dfrac{9}{4}$

   a. If $a + c > b + c$, then $a > b$.
   b. If $a > b$ and $b > c$, then $a > c$.
   c. If $ac > bc$ and $c > 0$, then $a > b$.
   d. If $ac > bc$ and $c < 0$, then $a < b$.

Another CLAST objective expected of Florida sophomore related to generalizations is inferring relations and making predictions from studying experiments in probability and statistics. Problems 110 and 111 illustrate this objective

110. A tetrahedron has four sides.
There are four possible outcomes when rolling one tetrahedron.
There are sixteen (4^2) possible outcomes when rolling two tetrahedrons.
There are sixty-four (4^3) possible outcomes when rolling three tetrahedrons.
Which expression below shows the number of possible outcomes for rolling n tetrahedrons when n represents a whole number greater than 1?

   a. n^4 b. 4^4 c. 4^n d. 2^n
   e. none are correct

111. Study the examples illustrating ways of combining objects two at a time.

3 objects	4 objects	5 objects	
(a,b,c)	(a,b,c,d)	(a,b,c,d,e)	
(a,b)	(a,b)	(a,b)	(b,e)
(a,c)	(a,c)	(a,c)	(c,d)
(b,c)	(a,d)	(a,d)	(c,e)
	(b,c)	(a,e)	(d,e)
	(b,d)	(b,c)	
	(c,d)	(b,d)	

Select the option that gives the number of ways of combining seven objects two at a time.

   a. 14   b. 15   c. 21   d. 28

Another generalization competency expected of students is the ability to identify the form of an argument. The type of knowledge needed to demonstrate this skill is shown in Problem 112.

112. Read each of the following valid arguments. Then select the symbolic form of the reasoning pattern illustrated by both arguments.

Sue will be a freshman or take math and Sue is not a freshman. Therefore she is taking math.

Ely is going to lose a race or go sailing, and he has won the race. As a result, he went sailing.

a.	p or q	b.	p and q	c.	p and q	d.	p or q
	not p		not q		q		q
	so, q		so, not p		so, p		so, not p

Students will need to demonstrate the ability to generalize and select correct generalizations in logical reasoning when needed to transform statements without affecting their meaning. Problem 113 illustrates this objective.

113. Following are three generalizations.
1. "If p then q" and "if not q then not p" are equivalent.
2. "If p then not q" and "not both p and q" are equivalent.
3. The statements "not (p or q)" and "not p and not q" are equivalent.

Which generalization above could be helpful in determining the equivalence of the two statements below?

- If x is even, then x^2 is even.
- If x^2 is not even, then x is not even.

114. Select the rule of logical equivalence that shows statement (a) is equal to statement (b).

a. All dogs are not rabid.　　b. none of the dogs are rabid.

1. "If p then q" is equivalent to "if not q then not p."
2. "not (not p)" is equivalent to "p."
3. "Not all are p" is equivalent to "some are not p."
4. "All are not p" is equivalent to "none are p."

Demonstrating the ability to solve problems in arithmetic relating to real world problems which do not require the use of variables is a requirement for Florida sophomores. Problem 115 shows a typical problem.

115. The price of a refrigerator is $320 but it is on sale for 30% off. The refrigerator is also available for a markup of 30% above the wholesale price of $184. Which is the better deal?

   a. $320 with a discount of 30%   b. $184 with a markup of 30%
   c. none are correct

> *Florida students are expected to solve problems involving the structure and logic of arithmetic. Nos. 116-117 illustrate this competency.*

116. How many whole numbers leave a remainder of 3 when divided into 66 and a remainder of 2 when divided into 23.

   a. 2   b. 3   c. 4   d. none

117. What size is the smallest positive whole number that leaves a remainder of 3 when divided by 5 and is evenly divisible by both 2 and 6?

   a. between 5 and 10   b. between 15 and 20   c. between 35 and 40
   d. between 75 and 80   e. none are correct

> *Problem 118 illustrates the competency of solving real world problems using perimeters, areas, and volumes of geometric figures.*

118. A rectangular roof measuring 40 feet by 30 feet has a square porch 9 feet long on a side extending from one side. The roof material cost is $70 for bundles covering 100 square feet and the labor cost for the roof is $275. What is the total cost of the labor and material to roof the building?

   a. $345   b. $1,115   c. $1185   d. $275
   e. none are correct

> *The CLAST objective of using the Pythagorean theorem to solve problems in geometry is shown by problem 119.*

119. A ship is heading East at 8 miles per hour across the Gulf Stream which is flowing North at 6 miles per hour. After 2 hours, how far has the ship traveled?

   a. 20 miles   b. 28 miles   c. 14 miles   d. 10 miles
   e. $\sqrt{28}$ miles   f. none are correct

Another problem-solving competency needed by Florida students is to solve problems involving algebra exclusive of geometric formulas. Numbers 120-122 illustrate this competency.

120. To find an estimate of the number of bass in a lake, rangers tagged 50 bass and released them in the lake. Then they netted 400 bass and found that 40 of them were tagged. What is a reasonable estimate of the number of bass in the lake?

a. 5   b. 50   c. 500   d. 5000   e. none are correct

121. Office equipment was purchased for $3,000 and is assumed to have a scrap value of $200 after 10 years. Assuming that it depreciates at the same rate each year, what is the value of the equipment after 4 years?

a. $1600   b. $1120   c. $1880   d. $2800

122. A driver leaves 140 feet of skid marks after braking to avoid an accident and the length of the skid marks varies directly as the square of the car's speed and at 30 mph skid marks are normally 40 feet long, how fast was the car traveling?

a. about 45 mph.   b. about 55 mph.   c. about 75 mph.
d. about 65 mph.   e. none are correct

Solving problems involving the structure and logic of algebra is a Florida competency as shown by problems 123 and 124.

123. The sum of a number and 4 more than twice the number is 32. Which equation could be used to find the number?

a. $x + 8x = 32$ c. $x - (4 + 2x) = 32$
b. $x + 2x = 32$ d. $x + 4 + 2x = 32$

124. Which of the following statements is false for every non-zero integer x?

a. $\dfrac{7}{x} > 0$ c. $\dfrac{2}{x} = 1$

b. $\dfrac{8}{x} = \dfrac{43}{32}$ d. $\dfrac{9}{x} = 0$

Real world problems involving the statistical concept of the normal curve is a competency illustrated by number 125.

125. Using the following table, solve the problem below.

Standard deviation above mean	Portion of area between mean and indicated standard deviation above the mean
.00	.000
.25	.099
.50	.192
.75	.273
1.00	.341
1.25	.394
1.50	.433
1.75	.460
2.00	.477
2.25	.488
2.50	.494
2.75	.497
3.00	.499

A college finds that the data on an achievement test for entering freshmen is normally distributed and has a mean score of 60 with a standard deviation of 6. If it admits any student who scores 54 or above, approximately what proportion of the applicants will be refused admission?

a. 34%   b. 16%   c. 84%   d. 68%   e. none are correct

Another competency in the area of probability and statistics is to find the probability of an event occurring in an experiment. Problems 126-127 shows test items for this competency.

126. Two people are to be drawn randomly from a group consisting of 50 people with half of them women and the rest men. What is the probability that both of them are women or both are men?

a. $2 \times \frac{1}{2} \times \frac{1}{2}$ b. $2 \times \frac{25}{50} \times \frac{24}{49}$ c. $2 \times \frac{25}{50} \times \frac{25}{50}$ d. $\frac{25}{50} \times \frac{24}{49}$

127. The odds that Lanie will get the job she wants is 5:8. With these odds, what is the probability that she will <u>not</u> get the job she wants?

a. $\frac{5}{8}$ b. $\frac{5}{3}$ c. $\frac{3}{5}$ d. $\frac{8}{13}$

Mathematics Test A

Drawing conclusions from a set of facts is another problem solving competency that involves logical reasoning. Problems 128-129 are illustrations of this objective.

128. Study the information below. Select the conclusion that is warranted by the facts given.

If you are a lawyer, you will be successful. If you are a doctor, you are successful. You are a lawyer and an accountant.

a. You will be successful
b. You will be a failure

c. You will not be successful
d. none of these are warranted.

129. Study the information below. Select the conclusion that is warranted by the facts given.

All lawyers are intelligent. Some intelligent people like to go to the opera. Bill likes to go to the opera.

a. Bill is a lawyer.
b. Bill is not a lawyer.
c. All people who like the opera are lawyers.
d. Some people who like the opera are lawyers.
e. none are logical conclusions.

Contributed by Florida A&M University

108

MATHEMATICS TEST B

Following is another sample test on the mathematics/computational competencies. It is strongly suggested that this test be taken only after any errors on Test A have been studied and corrected.

Sample B is much longer than the actual CLAST test because it includes a number of questions on each competency. The sequence of questions in Sample B is the same as the sequence in Sample A.

*Although Sample Test B covers the same competencies as Test A, the questions are significantly different. This is because each math competency can be tested in a number of different ways. Some of these ways are shown in Test A, but others are illustrated in Test B. It is highly recommended that a serious student solve **all** the problems in both tests to ensure readiness for the actual CLAST test.*

COLLEGE LEVEL SKILLS IN COMPUTATION   Form B

1. Add: $\frac{2}{3} + \frac{1}{2}$

    a. $1\frac{1}{6}$ b. $\frac{3}{5}$ c. $\frac{3}{6}$ d. $\frac{1}{2}$ e. none are correct

2. Subtract: $7\frac{5}{6} - \frac{1}{3}$

    a. $7\frac{4}{3}$ b. $7\frac{1}{2}$ c. $7\frac{4}{6}$ d. $7\frac{2}{3}$ e. none are correct

3. Multiply: $\frac{3}{4} \times 1\frac{1}{5}$

    a. $1\frac{3}{20}$ b. $3\frac{3}{20}$ c. $1\frac{19}{20}$ d. $\frac{9}{10}$ e. none are correct

4. Divide: $4\frac{2}{3} \div \frac{1}{3}$

    a. $\frac{20}{9}$ b. $\frac{5}{9}$ c. $\frac{2}{9}$ d. 14   e. none are correct

5. Add: .623 + 4.42

    a. 5.043   b. 1.045   c. 10.45   d. 104.5   e. 4.043
    f. none are correct

6. Subtract: 106.2 - 17.08

    a. 89.28   b. 89.12   c. .646   d. 64.6   e. 88.22
    f. none are correct

7. Multiply: 19.6 x 2.5

    a. 49   b. 4900   c. 4.9   d. 490   e. none are correct

8. Divide: 0.248 ÷ .4

    a. 620   b. 62   c. 6.2   d. .62   e. none are correct

9. Round off to the nearest kilogram (kgm): 54.2 kilograms

    a. 54 kgm   b. 55 kgm   c. 50 kgm   d. 60 kgm   e. none are correct

10. Round off to the nearest hundredth of a centimeter: 6.4852 cm

    a. 6.5 cm b. 6.49 cm c. 6.48 cm d. 6.4 cm e. none are correct

11. Round the measurement of the pictured object to the nearest $\frac{1}{2}$ inch.

    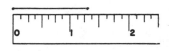

    a. $1\frac{1}{4}$ inch   b. $1\frac{1}{2}$ inch   c. 1 inch   d. $1\frac{3}{8}$ inch

    e. none are correct

12. Find the volume of a room 25 feet long, 30 feet wide, and 8 feet high.

    a. 6,000 ft.   b. 6,000 cu. ft.   c. 758 cu. ft.   d. 63 cu. ft.

    e. none are correct

13. What is the surface area of a rectangular solid that is 9 centimeters by 4 centimeters by 12 centimeters (cm)?

    a. 432 sq. cm   b. 432 cu. cm   c. 384 sq. cm   d. 384 cu. cm

14. What is the area of a circle that has a diameter of 6 cm?

    a. 6π cm   b. 27π sq. cm   c. 36π sq. cm   d. 9π sq. cm

15. What is the volume in liters (l) of a flask that will hold 1,275 milliliters?

    a. 12.75 l   b. 1.275 l   c. 127.5 l   d. 0.1275 l

16. Add: $3\sqrt{2} - 5\sqrt{2} - 8$

    a. $-2\sqrt{2} - 8$ b. $-10\sqrt{2}$ c. $-6\sqrt{2}$ d. -10

    e. none are correct

17. Multiply: $\sqrt{2} \times \sqrt{12}$

    a. $\sqrt{24}$ b. $2\sqrt{6}$ c. $4\sqrt{6}$ d. $6\sqrt{2}$ e. $6\sqrt{4}$

18. Subtract: $\sqrt{45} - \sqrt{80}$

   a. $-\sqrt{35}$ b. $\sqrt{-35}$ c. $7\sqrt{5}$ d. $-\sqrt{5}$ e. none are correct

19. Divide: $12 \div 4\sqrt{3}$

   a. $\dfrac{\sqrt{3}}{3}$ b. $\dfrac{3}{\sqrt{3}}$ c. $\dfrac{\sqrt{3}}{4}$ d. $\sqrt{3}$ e. $4\sqrt{30}$

   f. $3\sqrt{\dfrac{12}{3}}$

20. Simplify: $\dfrac{1}{2} - 8(\dfrac{1}{4} + 1)$

   a. $-3\dfrac{1}{2}$ b. $-\dfrac{1}{2}$ c. $-9\dfrac{1}{2}$ d. $-9\dfrac{3}{8}$ e. none are correct

21. Simplify: $3a^2 \div a + 2a \times 2 - 5a$

   a. $2a$ b. $-2a$ c. $5a$ d. $-5a$ e. none are correct

22. Simplify: $(8t) - (3) \times (2t) + (5t)$

   a. $12t$ b. $35t^2$ c. $15t$ d. $7t$ e. none are correct

23. Use scientific notation to find the answer: $\dfrac{5.6 \times 10^{-3}}{1.4 \times 10^{-2}}$

   a. 4×10^{-5} b. 4×10^{-1} c. 4×10^{5} d. 4.2×10^{-1}
   e. 4.2×10^{1} f. none are correct

24. Compute and give the answer in scientific notation. $2.5 \times 10^{3} + 1.2 \times 10^{4}$

   a. 3.7×10^{7} b. 1.45×10^{6} c. 1.45×10^{4} d. 2.62×10^{3}
   e. none are correct

25. If $-2x - 3 \leq 3x + 7$, then

   a. $x \leq -2$ b. $x \leq 2$ c. $x \geq -2$ d. $x \leq 4$ e. none are correct

112

26. If $7x + 3 = 9x - 5$, then X = ?

    a. $- 4$　　　b. 1　　　　c. -1　　　d. 4　　　　e. $-\frac{1}{8}$

27. If $-\frac{3}{4}x = 16$, then X = ?

    a. $-21\frac{1}{3}$　　b. -12　　　　c. $\frac{64}{3}$　　　　d. $21\frac{1}{3}$

28. If $5[x - (2x - 3)] = 2(x - 3)$, then X = ?

    a. $\frac{18}{5}$　　　b. 3　　　c. -18　　　d. 4　　　　e. none are correct

29. Use the relation $y = (x - 6)^2$ to find y when x = 0.

    a. -6　　　b. -12　　　c. -36　　　d. 36　　　e. none are correct

30. Use the relation $a = b^2 - 2b - 3$ to find a when b = -2.

    a. -3　　　b. 11　　　c. -5　　　d. 5　　　e. none are correct

31. The formula for converting a Fahrenheit temperature to Celcius is
    $C = \frac{5}{9}(F - 32)$.　What is the temperature on the Celcius scale
    when the Fahrenheit temperature is 68°?

    a. 4.6°　　　b. 4.66°　　　c. 20°　　　　d. none are correct

32. The formula for converting a Celcius temperature to Fahrenheit is
    $F = \frac{9}{5}C + 32$.　What is the Fahrenheit temperature when the Celcius
    temperature is 30°?

    a. 86°　　　b. 111.6°　　　c. 110.6°　　　d. none are correct

33. The formula for the sales price of an object is $P = C + MC$.　The
    cost (C) of an object is $12 and the markup (M) is 40%.　What is the
    sales price (P)?

    a. $52　　　　b. $492　　　　c. $12.48　　　　d. $16.80
    e. none are correct

113

34. The graph on the right represents the grade record of the students in a school. How many less students make B's than C's?

    a. 60
    d. 40
    b. -20
    e. 20
    c. 100

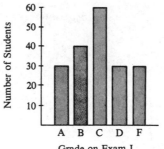

Grade on Exam I

35. The graph at the right shows the average price of gasoline in cents in an area of the country between 1973 and 1979. Which two consecutive years had the greatest increase in cost?

    a. 1973 and 1974
    b. 1974 and 1975
    c. 1973 and 1977
    d. 1976 and 1977
    e. none of these

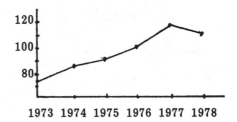

36. The graph at the right shows the distribution of grades on an examination given to a sophomore class of 500 students. What percent of the students earned a grade above a C?

    a. 70%
    d. 80%
    b. 90%
    e. 40%
    c. 200 students

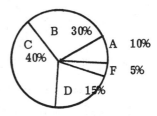

37. Find the <u>mean</u> of the numbers 7, 4, 10, 13, 6, 7, 5, 6, 5, 7.
    a. 5   b. 6   c. 7   d. 8   e. none are correct

38. Find the <u>median</u> of the numbers 1, 3, 5, 4, 6, 5, 6, 6, 9, 10.
    a. 4.5   b. 5   c. 5.5   d. 6   e. none are correct

39. Find the <u>mode</u> of the numbers 13, 12, 12, 15, 10, 13, 11, 17, 13, 15.

    a. 12   b. 12.5   c. 13   d. 13.5   e. 14

40. Each of the two digit whole numbers less than 20 are written on a separate slip of paper and dropped into a box. If one slip is drawn randomly from the box and it is known that it is an odd number, what is the sample space for this experiment?

    a. $\{10,11,12,13,14,15,16,17,18,19\}$ b. $\{10,12,14,16,18\}$
    c. $\{x|9 < x \le 20\}$ d. $\{11,13,15,17,19\}$ e. none are correct

41. Sets A, B, C, and U are related as shown in the diagram. Assume that none of the regions are empty. Select the answer/s that is/are true.

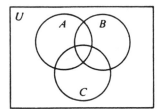

   1. An element which is a member of set B is also a member of A.
   2. If an element is not a member of either set C or set B, but is a member of set A then it is a member of U.
   3. An element is a member of set A only if it is a member of U.

    a. 1 only   b. 2 only   c. 3 only   d. 1 and 2 only
    e. 2 and 3 only   f. 1 and 3 only   g. all are true

42. Sets A, B, C, and U are related as shown in the diagram. Assume that none of the regions are empty. Select the answer that is true.

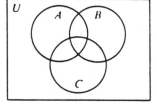

   1. An element which is a member of set A and set B is also a member of set C.
   2. An element is a member of U if it is a member of A.
   3. No elements are members of all three sets.

    a. 1 only   b. 2 only   c. 3 only   d. 1 and 2 only
    e. 1 and 3   f. 2 and 3 only   g. all are correct

43. Select the equivalent expression for $3^2 + 4^2$.

    a. $(3)(2) + (4)(2)$ b. $(3 + 4)^2$ c. $(3 + 4)^4$ d. $(3)(3) + (4)(4)$

44. Select the equivalent expression for $(3^2)^4$

    a. $3^2 \times 3^2 \times 3^2 \times 3^2$ b. $(3 \times 2)^4$ c. 3^{16} d. 3^6

45. Select the place value associated with the underlined digit.

    54.0<u>3</u>7 (base eight)

    a. 8^2 b. $\frac{1}{8}$ c. $\frac{1}{8^2}$ d. $\frac{1}{8^3}$ e. none are correct

46. Find the base-ten equivalent to 133 (base-five.)

    a. 55   b. 43   c. 40   d. 41   e. none are correct

47. Identify the equivalent expression to 0.02.

    a. .2%   b. 2%   c. 20%   d. 0.2%   e. .02%

48. Identify the equivalent expression to 76%.

    a. .076   b. 0.76   c. 7.6   d. 76   e. 7600

49. Identify the equivalent expression to $\frac{9}{16}$.

    a. .0563%   b. .563%   c. 5.63%   d. 56.3%   e. none are correct

50. Choose the symbol for $- \frac{12}{18}$ [ ] $- \frac{4}{6}$.

    a. $<$ b. $>$ c. $=$

51. Choose the symbol for $(\frac{4}{3})^2$ [ ] $\frac{4}{3}$.

    a. $<$ b. $>$ c. $=$

52. Choose the symbol for $10.\overline{345}$ [ ] $10.3\overline{45}$

  a. <   b. >   c. =

53. Choose the symbol for -0.25 [ ] $\frac{1}{3}$

  a. <   b. >   c. =

54. Choose the symbol for 8.052 [ ] 8.1

  a. <   b. >   c. =

55. The diagram on the right
shows lines in the same plane.
Line m_3 is vertical.
Select the true statement/s.
  1. Lines m_2 and m_4 are neither
     intersecting nor perpendicular.
  2. Lines m_3 and m_4 are not
     intersecting and horizontal.
  3. Lines m_1 and m_2 are parallel
     and horizontal.

  a. 1 only   b. 2 only   c. 3 only   d. 1 and 2 only
  e. 1 and 3 only f. 2 and 3 only g. none are correct

56. For the figure at the right, which
statement(s) is/are true?
Lines m_1 and m_2 are parallel.

  1. $\angle C \cong \angle I$
  2. $\angle K$ measures 60°
  3. $\angle K$ is supplementary to $\angle A$.

  a. 1 only   b. 2 only   c. 3 only   d. 1,2 only
  e. 1,2,3 only   f. 2,3 only   g. 1,3 only

117

57. For the figure on the right, which state-
    ment is true given that m_1 is parallel
    to m_2?

    1. m $\angle$F = 60°.
    2. $\angle$F $\cong$ $\angle$B.
    3. $\angle$K is supplemental to $\angle$A.
    4. Since m $\angle$J = 60°, m $\angle$ A = 30°

    a. 1 only   b. 2 only   c. 3 only
    d. 4 only   e. 1 and 3
    f. 2 and 3   g. none are correct

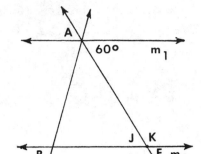

58. Select the geometric figure that possesses **all** of the following
    characteristics.

    1. three sides   2. angles may not be congruent
    3. two angles are complementary

    a. isosceles triangle   b. equilateral triangle
    c. scalene triangle   d. right triangle

59. Select the answer with the figures that have **all** of the following
    characteristics. The figure is a quadrilateral and the diagonals may
    not be equal but the opposite sides are parallel and equal. The angles
    may not be 90°
    1. square   2. rhombus   3. rectangle   4. trapezoid

    a. 1 only   b. 2 only   c. 3 only   d. 4 only   e. 1 and 2 only
    f. 2 and 4 only   g. 3 and 4 only   h. 2 and 4 only

60. Which of the following is an obtuse angle?
    a.   b.   c.   d.

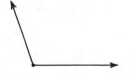   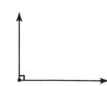

61. Choose the figure(s) that is(are) trapezoid(s).

1. 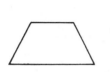 2. 3. 4. 5.

a. 1 only   b. 2 only   c. 3 only   d. 4 only   e. 5 only
f. 1 and 2 only   g. 3 and 4 only   h. All are correct

62. For the triangles on the right identify the answer/s below.

1. $\angle BAC \cong \angle EDC$

2. $\dfrac{AB}{DE} = \dfrac{BE}{EC}$

3. $\angle EDC \cong \angle ECD$

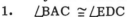

a. 1 only   b. 2 only   c. 3 only   d. 1 and 2 only
e. 1 and 3 only   f. 2 and 3 only   g. none are correct

63. Which of the sets of pictured triangles contain/s similar triangles?

1. 2. 3.

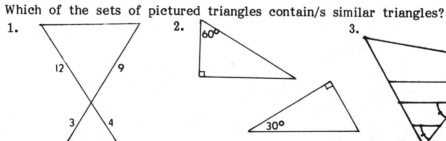

a. 1 only   b. 2 only   c. 3 only   d. 1 and 2 only
e. 1 and 3 only   f. 2 and 3   g. all are correct

119

64. Which of the statements 1,2, or 3 is/are true for the pictured triangles with $\angle A \cong \angle E$?
The notation m($\overline{AB}$) denotes the measure or length of $\overline{AB}$ and not the segment AB itself.

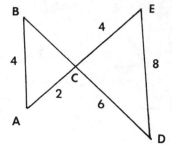

1. $\dfrac{DC}{CB} = \dfrac{ED}{AC}$
2. m($\overline{BC}$) = 3
3. $\angle B \cong \angle E$

a. 1 only   b. 2 only   c. 3 only   d. 1 and 2 only
e. 1 and 3 only   f. 2 and 3 only   g. 1,2,3

65. Identify the type of measure needed for segment $\overline{DC}$ in the figure shown.

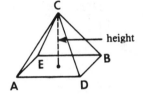

a. linear   d. square
b. cubic   e. face
c. metric

66. Identify the type of measure needed for the surface area of a cube.

a. linear   b. square   c. cubic   d. surface   e. metric

67. Identify the type of measure needed for the region X, the interior of the figure.

a. linear
b. square
c. cubic
d. surface
e. metric

68. Identify the property of operation illustrated below:
    $$-(a + 2b) + (a + 2b) = 0$$

    a. Associative property of multiplication
    b. Associative property of addition
    c. Commutative property of addition
    d. Commutative property of multiplication
    e. Distributive property of multiplication over addition
    f. Identity property of multiplication
    g. Inverse property of addition

69. Identify the property of operation illustrated below:
    $$(2a + 3)(3) = 3(2a + 3)$$

    a. Associative property of multiplication
    b. Associative property of addition
    c. Commutative property of addition
    d. Commutative property of multiplication
    e. Distributive property of multiplication over addition
    f. Identity property of multiplication
    g. Inverse property of addition

70. Which statement illustrates the inverse property of multiplication?

    a. $3(2a) = (3 \times 2)a$
    b. $(a)(b) + c = c + (b)(a)$
    c. $a \times b = b \times a$
    d. $(2)(b) + (2)(d) = 2(b + d)$
    e. $(\frac{1}{b}) \times b = 1$ if $b \neq 0$
    f. $-a \times a = 0$

71. Choose the equivalent expression for: $5 + (7 + a)$.

    a. $(5 \times 7)a$ b. $(5 + 7) + a$ c. $12(a)$ d. $35(a)$
    e. $5(7 + a)$ f. $5(12)(a)$ g. $(5 + 7)(a)$

72. Determine which of the following equations or inequalities have (-1) as a solution?
    1. $(x - 1)(x - 2) \geq 3$ 2. $|x - 1| = -2$ 3. $3x < 2x + 1$
    4. $x^2 - x - 2 = 0$
    Which option below identifies every statement that has (-1) as a solution and only that (those) statement(s).

    a. 1 only   b. 2 only   c. 3 only   d. 4 only
    e. 1, 3, and 4 only   f. 1, 2, and 3 only   g. All are correct

121

73. Determine which of the following equations or inequalities have $(-\frac{3}{5})$ as a solution?

    1. $\frac{-5}{3} x = -1$ 2. $(2x - 1)(x + 5) < 2$ 3. $x - \frac{1}{2} = -\frac{11}{10}$

    Which option below identifies <u>every</u> statement that has $(-\frac{3}{5})$ as a solution and <u>only</u> that (those) statement(s).

    a. 1 only   b. 2 only   c. 3 only   d. 1 and 2 only
    e. 1 and 3 only   f. 2 and 3 only   g. none are correct

74. Three people can make eight computers in five days. Let R represent the number of computers they can make in 24 days. Select the correct proportion for these conditions.

    a. $\frac{8}{5} = \frac{R}{24}$ b. $\frac{8}{5} = \frac{24}{R}$ c. $\frac{8}{3} = \frac{R}{24}$ d. $\frac{3}{8} = \frac{24}{R}$

75. The area of a rug is held constant while the width and length change and if the length is 12 meters when the width is 4 meters, select the statement of the condition when the width is 5.

    a. $\frac{5}{12} = \frac{L}{4}$ b. $\frac{4}{12} = \frac{5}{L}$ c. $\frac{12}{L} = \frac{5}{4}$ d. $\frac{4}{12} = \frac{L}{5}$
    e. none are correct

76. Which shaded region identifies the portion of the plane in which $x \geq 0$ and $y \leq 0$?

    a.   b.   c.   d.

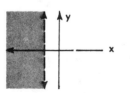 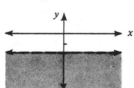 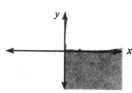

122

77. Which option/s give/s the conditions that correspond to the shaded region of the plane shown at the right?

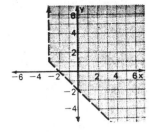

   a. $y \geq 0$ and $y \geq -3$
   b. $y \geq -3$ or $x + y \leq -2$
   c. $x \geq -3$ and $x + y \leq -2$
   d. $x \geq -3$ and $x + y \geq -2$
   e. $x \leq -3$ and $x + y \geq -2$

78. Which option gives the condition that corresponds to the graph on the right?

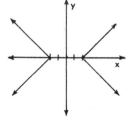

   a. $|x| = |y| + 2$
   b. $y = |x| + 2$
   c. $|y| = |x| + 2$
   d. $|x| = |y| - 2$

79. Which of the following statements is/are true for a set of scores that is normally distributed?
   1. The probability that a score falls within 1 standard deviation above or below the mean is approximately 68%.
   2. The probability that a score falls between 1 and 2 standard deviations above the mean is equal to the probability that a score falls between 2 and 3 standard deviations above the mean.
   3. About 10% of the scores are more than three standard deviation from the mean.
   4 The median score is different from the mean score.

   a. 1 only   b. 2 only   c. 3 only   d. 1 and 2 only   e. 1 and 3 only
   f. all are correct

80. The population of a college consists of $\frac{6}{10}$ Caucasian, $\frac{3}{10}$ Afro-American, and $\frac{1}{10}$ Hispanic. Which of the following samples is most representative of the school population?

	Caucasian	Afro-american	Hispanic	total
a.	840	140	420	1400
b.	344	240	66	650
c.	960	470	170	1600
d.	60	30	710	800
e.	none are correct			

81. A box contains 4 red balls, 2 black balls, and 3 green balls. Two balls are drawn at random and replaced after each draw. What is the probability that the first ball is red and the second ball is green?

a. $\frac{4}{27}$ b. $\frac{12}{81}$ c. $\frac{7}{9}$ d. $\frac{2}{9}$ e. $\frac{7}{72}$

82. A coin is tossed two times. What is the probability of not obtaining two tails?

a. 1   b. 0.75   c. 0.5   d. 0.25   e. 0

f. none are correct.

83. Select the correct negation of the statement:
"Sam is a barber or George is a butcher."

a. Sam is not a barber and George is not a butcher.
b. Sam is not a barber or George is not a butcher.
c. Sam is not a barber or George is a butcher.
d. Sam is a barber and George is not a butcher.
e. All are correct.

84. Select the statement that negates: "If Burt loafs, then he will fail.

a. Burt does not loaf and he will not fail.
b. If Burt does not loaf, then he will not fail.
c. If Burt does not fail, then he did not loaf.
d. Burt does not loaf or he will fail.
e. none are correct

85. Select the statement below which is **not** logically equivalent to "It is not true that both Sid is a girl and Gene is a boy."

a. Sid is not a girl and Gene is not a boy.
b. If Gene is a boy, then Sid is a not girl.
c. If Sid is a girl, then Gene is not a boy.
d. Sid is not a girl or Gene is not a boy.

86. Select the statement that is logically equivalent to:
"If a cow does give milk, then it is productive."

a. If a cow does not give milk, then it is not productive.
b. If a cow is productive, then it does not give milk.
c. If a cow is not productive, then it does not give milk.
d. A cow gives milk, if it is productive.

87. Select the statement/s below which is/are **not** logically equivalent to: "John and Jean are students."

    1. John is not a student and Jean is not a student.
    2. John is not a student or Jean is not a student.
    3. If John is a student, then Jean is a student.
    4. It is not true that both John is not a student or Jean is not a student.

    a. 1 only   b. 2 only   c. 3 only   d. 4 only
    e. 1,2, and 3 only   f. 2 and 3 only   g. All are not equivalent

88. Select the statement which is equivalent to "All geometric figures are rectangles."

    a. Some geometric figures are not rectangles.
    b. There is no rectangle that is a geometric figure.
    c. No rectangle is not a geometric figure.
    d. No geometric figure is not a rectangle.
    e. Some geometric figures are rectangles.

89. Select the inverse of the statement "If Janie earns an A, George goes to college."

    a. If George goes to college, Janie earns an A.
    b. If George does not go to college, Janie does not earn an A.
    c. If Janie does not earn an A, George does not go to college.
    d. If George goes to college, Janie does not earn an A.

90. Read the requirements and each applicant's application for obtaining financial aid. Then identify the applicant that qualifies for aid.

    To qualify for financial aid, a student must have at least a "C" average in high school, have a family income of less than $25,000 per year, and register for at least 12 hours of classes.

    Ernie has a B average, has a family income of $28,500 per year, and has registered for 15 hours of classes.

    Sue's parents earn $18,800 per year and she made $2,450 last year. She made C's or better in high school. She has registered for 12 hours of classes.

    Bob's dad makes $19,500 a year, his mother $5,000, and he earned $1,500 last year. He has signed up for 13 hours for the fall and made a 3.4 average in high school.

    a. Ernie   b. Sue   c. Bob   d. none are qualified

Mathematics Test B

91. Given that: All horses have four legs and
                 all furry animals have four legs.
    Determine which conclusions can be logically deduced.

    a. All furry animals are horses.   d. Some horses are furry animals.
    b. All horses are furry animals.   e. Some furry animals are horses.
    c. No furry animals are horses.   f. none are correct

92. All of the following arguments have true conclusions, but not all of the
    arguments are valid. Select the argument/s that are **not** valid.
    1. If Billy can follow a scent, then he can catch the fox. Bill can't
        catch the fox. Therefore Billy cannot follow a scent.
    2. If Billy can follow a scent, then he can catch the fox. He caught
        the fox. Therefore, Billy can follow a scent.
    3. If Billy can follow a scent, then he can catch the fox. Billy can't
        follow a scent. Therefore he cannot catch the fox.

    a. 1 only   b. 2 & 3 only   c. 2 only   d. 3 only   e. 1 & 3 only

93. Which of the following arguments is/are fallacious?
    1. Ralph can run fast or he can swim and it's known that he can run fast.
        Therefore he cannot swim.
    2. Florida is Ford country and Ocala is in Florida. As a result,
        Ocala belongs to Ford.
    3. A famous physicist stated that vitamin B1 will cure a common
        disease and Will takes large doses of the vitamin. Therefore he
        will not get the disease.

    a. 1 and 2 only   b. 1 and 3 only   c. 2 and 3 only   d. 1 only
    e. 2 only   f. 3 only   g. All are correct
                                                  (fallacious)

94. Which of the following arguments is/are fallacious?
    1. Senator Williams can obtain advance information on good real
        estate investments and David is the Senator's assistant. Therefore
        David can obtain the same information.
    2. Bill was asked if he had ever stolen anything and he replied that
        he had not. Therefore he is not a criminal.
    3. Karen will not buy a car because if Karen gets a job, she will buy
        a car and she did not get a job.

        a. 1 only   b. 2 only   c. 3 only   d. 1 and 2 only
        e. 1 and 3 only   f. 2 and 3 only   g. All are correct
                                                      (fallacious)

126

95. Which of the following arguments is/are **not** fallacious?
    1. If Tom works for a TV studio, he will make a lot of money and he made a lot of money. As a result, he worked for a TV studio.
    2. A certain model of a manufacturers car is well-made and Ivetta bought another model from the same manufacturer. Therefore it is well-made.
    3. Sheryl does not have much money because she was poor in school and poor people do not have much money.

    a. 1 only   b. 2 only   c. 3 only   d. 1 and 2 only
    e. 1 and 3 only   f. 2 and 3 only   g. All are fallacious

96. Which of the following illustrates a **proof by contradiction**?
    1. Saul does buy a car because we know that
        i) if Saul had money, he would buy a car, and
        ii) Saul had money.
    2. Mike did not study as needed because we know that
        i) on Saturday, Mike needed to work 8 hours, play tennis 3 hours, sleep 8 hours and study 6 hours, and
        ii) he worked, played tennis and slept the needed number of hours, and $8 + 3 + 8 = 19$ and $24 - 19 = 5$, there would have to be more than 24 hours in a day.
    3. Dave went to town because we know that
        i) he was going to town and to school, and
        ii) he did go to school.

    a. 1 only   b. 2 only   c. 3 only   d. 1 and 3 only
    e. 1 and 2 only   f. 2 and 3 only   g. All are correct
    h. none are correct

97. Which of the following tasks are best suited for a computer?
    1. Jobs requiring organizational ability
    2. Jobs requiring speed.   5. Jobs requiring good judgement.
    3. Repetitive tasks.   6. Jobs requiring a large memory.
    4. Jobs requiring simulation.

    a. 2 and 6 only   b. 1 and 2 only   c. 2, 3, 4, and 6 only
    d. 1, 3, 4, and 5 only   e. All are correct

98. Computers have the ability to do repetitive tasks easily. Which of the following tasks would take advantage of this computer ability?
    1. Simulating the path of a satellite.
    2. Checking the figures on income tax forms for the citizens in a state.
    3. Turning on a bathroom light.
    4. Aiming a missile.
    5. Drawing 3-dimensional graphs of airplane parts.

99. Select the option in which a computer is used to the detriment of society.
    1. To record retirement information
    2. Bill changed a bank's program so that $1,000 was added to each depositor's account.
    3. Sally entered a company's computer and made it deliver thousands of dollars worth of building material to her property.
    4. To record lists of citizens who criticize the government.

    a. 1 and 3 only   b. 1, 2, and 4 only   c. 2, 3 and 4 only
    d. 1, 3, 4 only   e. All are a detriment

100. Look for a common linear relationship between the numbers in each pair. Then identify the missing term.

$$(8,2), \quad (4,1), \quad (2,\tfrac{1}{2}), \quad (1,\tfrac{1}{4}), \quad (.0012,.0003), \quad (.01,\underline{\quad})$$

    a. .25   b. .025   c. 25   d. .0025   e. .004

101. Identify the missing term in the following arithmetic progression.

$$-5, \quad -2, \quad 1, \quad 4, \quad \underline{\quad}$$

    a. 5   b. 6   c. 7   d. 8

102. To mentally simplify the expression below , which property or properties below should be used to complete the simplification in the **least** number of steps?

$$\frac{1}{2} + (\frac{5}{7} + 9\frac{1}{2})$$

    a. commutative and associative properties of addition
    b. distributive property
    c. associative property of addition and distributive property
    d. Distributive property and commutative property of addition
    e. none are correct

103. Select the property of operation illustrated in this equation.

$$.25 + (1.33 + .75) = .25 + (.75 + 1.33)$$

a. $a + (b + c) = (b + c) + a$
b. $a + b = b + a$
c. $a(b + c) = ab + ac$
d. $a + (b + c) = (a + b) + c$

104. Select the property or properties of operation(s) illustrated in this equation. The letter "x" is used to indicate multiplication.

$$2(2x7^5) = (2x2)7^5$$

a. distributive property and commutative property of multiplication
b. commutative property of multiplication
c. associative property of multiplication
d. associative property of multiplication and distributive property

105. Study the figure showing a rectangle and select the formula for computing the perimeter of the figure.

a. perimeter = 4h + 4k
b. perimeter = 2h + 2k
c. perimeter = 16hk
d. perimeter = 4hk

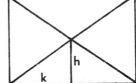

106. Study the figure consisting of a right circular cone on top of a right circular cylinder. Then select the formula that will give the total volume of the figure.

a. Volume = $\pi r^2 h + \pi r^2$

b. Volume = $\pi r^2 h + \frac{1}{3}\pi r^2 h$

c. Volume = $2\pi r + \pi rh$

d. Volume = $2\pi r + \frac{1}{2}rh$

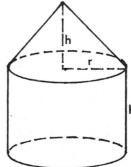

107. Study the figures on the right and select the correct formula for the area of a regular n-sided polygon.

a. A = nbh

3-sides: A $= \frac{1}{2}$ bh

b. A $= \frac{1}{2}$ nbh

4-sides: A = 2bh

c. A $= \frac{1}{3}$ nbh

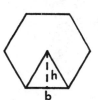

6-sides: A = 3bh

d. A $= \frac{n-2}{2}$ bh

108. Select the formulas needed for calculating the area of the figure which consists of a polygon and a semi-circle.

1. A $= 2 \pi r$

2. A $= \frac{1}{2} h(b_1 + b_2)$

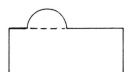

3. A $= \frac{1}{2} hb$

4. A $= \pi r^2$

5. A = LW

a. 1 and 2 only   b. 3 and 4 only   c. 4 and 5 only
d. 2 and 3 only   e. none are correct

109. Study the information given with the regular hexagons.

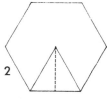

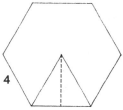

area = $\frac{3}{2}\sqrt{3}$ area = $6\sqrt{3}$ area = $24\sqrt{3}$

Calculate the area of a regular hexagon with a side equal to 8.

a. $24\sqrt{3}$ b. $96\sqrt{3}$ c. $48\sqrt{3}$ d. $72\sqrt{3}$

110. Study the following examples. The notation a x a means a multiplied by a.

$a^2 \times a^3 = (a \times a)(a \times a \times a) = a^5$

$a \times a^4 = a(a \times a \times a \times a) = a^5$

$(a^3)^2 \times (a^2) = (a^3 \times a^3) \times a^2 = a^8$

Determine which of the following appears to hold for all numbers a and all whole numbers x and y.

1. $(a^x)(a^y) = a^{x+y}$ 2. $(a^x)(a^y) = a^{xy}$ 3. $(a^x)(a^y) = (a^x)^y$

a. 1 only   b. 2 only   c. 3 only   d. 1 and 2 only
e. 1 and 3 only   f. 2 and 3 only   g. All are correct

111. Study the three examples: $X^2 \$ X^3 \& X^6 = X^{20}$

$X^4 \$ X^2 \& X^3 = X^{10}$

$X^4 \$ X^5 \& X^4 = X^{24}$

Select the equation that is compatible with the data above.

a. $X^a \$ X^b \& X^c = X^{a+b+c}$

b. $X^a \$ X^b \& X^c = X^{(a \times b)+c}$

c. $X^a \$ X^b \& X^c = X^{a+(b \times c)}$

d. $X^a \$ X^b \& X^c = X^{a \times b \times c}$

112. Select the property used to justify the following statement:

If $5 < x + 2 < 17$, then $3 < x < 15$.

a. If $a + b > c + b$, then $a > c$.
b. If $a > b$ and $b > c$, then $a > c$.
c. If $ac > bc$ and $c > 0$, then $a > b$.
d. If $ac > bc$ and $c < 0$, then $a < b$.

113. Select the property used to justify the following statement:

If $-2x > 7$, then $x < -\frac{7}{2}$

a. If $a + b > c + b$, then $a > c$.
b. If $a > b$ and $b > c$, then $a > c$.
c. If $ac > bc$ and $c > 0$, then $a > b$.
d. If $ac > bc$ and $c < 0$, then $a < b$.

114. Select the property used to justify the following statement:

If $x - 3 = 8$, then $x = 11$

a. If $a = b$, then $ac = bc$.
b. If $a = b$, then $a + c = b + c$.
c. If $ac > bc$ and $c > 0$, then $a > b$.
d. If $ac > bc$ and $c < 0$, then $a < b$.

115. Study the outcomes for tossing 1, 2, or 3 coins simultaneously.

1 coin	2 coins	3 coins	
H	HH	HHH	THH
T	HT	HHT	THT
	TH	HTH	TTH
	TT	HTT	TTT

If 5 coins were tossed simultaneously, how many possible arrangements of heads and tails would there be?

a. 12 c. 28
b. 16 d. 32

116. Study the examples illustrating the number of ways of combining one less than the number of objects in the original set.

3 objects (a,b,c) 2 at a time	4 objects (a,b,c,d) 3 at a time	5 objects (a,b,c,d,e) 4 at a time
(a,b)	(a,b,c)	(a,b,c,d)
(a,c)	(a,b,d)	(a,b,c,e)
(b,c)	(a,c,d)	(a,b,d,e)
	(b,c,d)	(a,c,d,e)
		(b,c,d,e)

How many 7 member sets can be combined from 8 objects?
a. 6   b. 7   c. 8   d. 9

117. Each of the following are valid arguments.

    If I study hard, I will do well. I did not do well. Therefore I did not study hard.

    If Sue is a freshman, then she will take math and Sue is not taking math. Therefore she is not a freshman.

Judging from the arguments above, which of the following are valid for all statement values of p and q?

a.   p   q
    not p
    so, not q

b.   p   q
    not q
    so, not p

c.   p   q
    q
    so, p

d.   p   q
    q
    so, not p

118. Which rule of logical equivalence below is helpful to change statement (a) into statement (b)?

a - Debby does not hate math or Vito does not like English.
b - If Debby hates math, Vito does not like English.

1. "If p, then q" and "if not q, then not p" are equivalent.
2. "If p, then not q" and "not p or not q" are equivalent.
3. The statements "not (p or q)" and "not p and not q" are equivalent.
4. The correct equivalence rule is not given.

119. A department store ordered 50 pairs of slacks that it sold for $20 each. They cost the store $15 apiece. It had to return 5 pair for credit and were charged $3 for each pair returned. How much profit was made on the pants?

a. $214   b. $210   c. $225   d. $325

120. In an effort to estimate the number of deer in a forest, rangers trapped 20 deer and found that 5 of them were tagged. Previously they had tagged 40 deer and released them. What is the most reasonable estimate of the number of deer in the forest?

a. 20   b. 200   c. 2,000   d. 160   e. 1,600
f. none are correct

121. What size is the smallest positive whole number that leaves a remainder of 3 when divided by 5 and is evenly divisible by both 2 and 6?

a. 48   b. 18   c. 12   d. 8   e. none are correct

122. A plumbing contractor needs to install a drain line as shown in the dotted line in the figure. It will cost $2,000 per hundred meters to install. What is the estimated cost of the line?

a. $2,000
b. $4,000
c. $6,000
d. $1,000,000
e. $10,000

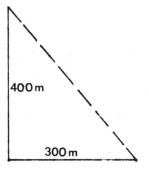

400 m

300 m

123. A rectangular floor measuring 20 feet by 30 feet has a square hole 8 feet long on a side in the center. The flooring material cost is $200 for bundles covering 100 square feet and the labor cost for the floor is $375. What is the total cost of the labor and material to build the floor?

a. $575   b. $1,375   c. $1,575   d. $1,775
e. none are correct

124. Computing equipment was purchased for $8,000 and is assumed to have a scrap value of $1,000 after 10 years. Assuming that it depreciates at the same rate each year, what is the value of the equipment after 3 years?

a. $2,100   b. $5,900   c. $6,900   d. $3,000
e. none are correct

125. A rectangular swimming pool is surrounded by a walk three feet wide. If the pool is 17 feet by 30 feet, what is the area of the walk?

    a. 318 sq. ft.   b. 510 sq. ft.   c. 282 sq. ft.   d. 828 sq. ft.

126. How loud is a sound 60 meters from the source if sound varies inversely with the square of the distance and at 20 meters the sound has a rating of 2 units.

    a. $\frac{1}{2}$ unit   b. $\frac{2}{9}$ units.   c. 3 units

    d. $\frac{1}{3}$ unit   e. none are correct

127. A circus erection manager is going to brace a 40 meter center pole of a tent with 4 cables fastened on the ground 9 meters from the bottom of the pole and extending to the top of the pole. How many meters of cable will be needed?

    a. 41 m   b. 49 m   c. 164 m   d. 196 m

128. Three times the sum of a number and 5 is 89. Which equation could be used to find the number?

    a. $3x + 5 = 89$ c. $8x = 89$
    b. $3(x+5) = 89$ d. $(3x) = 5 + 89$

129. The sum of two whole numbers is even. Which of the following statements is true about the two numbers?

    a. Both of the numbers may be even.
    b. Both of the numbers may be odd.
    c. One may be odd and the other one even.
    d. The difference between the two numbers may be odd.

130. Using the following table, solve the problem below.

Standard deviation above mean	Proportion of area between mean and indicated standard deviation above the mean
.00	.000
.25	.099
.50	.192
.75	.273
1.00	.341
1.25	.394
1.50	.433
1.75	.460
2.00	.477
2.25	.488
2.50	.494
2.75	.497
3.00	.499

A car manufacturer finds that the data on the length of time to the first repair on their new cars is normally distributed with a mean of 13 months and a standard deviation of 2 months. Approximately what percent of the cars will break down before being used 11 months?

a. 50%   b. 34%   c. 16%   d. 14%   e. 2%
e. none are correct

131. Two students are chosen at random for a scholarship from a group consisting of 6 Caucasians, 3 Hispanics, 7 Afro-Americans, and 2 Asian-Americans. What is the probability that they are both Asian-American or both Afro-Americans?

a. $\frac{2}{18} \times \frac{1}{17} + \frac{7}{18} \times \frac{6}{17}$ c. $2 \times \frac{9}{18}$

b. $\frac{2}{18} + \frac{7}{18}$ d. $\frac{2}{18} \times \frac{1}{18} \times \frac{7}{18} \times \frac{6}{18}$

e. none are correct.

132. The probability that Sam will <u>win</u> the election is $\frac{6}{7}$. With this probability, what are the odds he will <u>lose</u> the election?

a. 6:1   b. 1:6   c. 6:7   d. 7:6   e. 7:13

133. Study the information below. If a logical conclusion is given, select that conclusion. Otherwise indicate that none are warranted.

All presidents of large companies make a lot of money. All people that make a lot of money have several houses. Aga has three houses.

a. Aga makes a lot of money.
b. Aga does not make a lot of money.
c. Aga is the president of a large company.
d. none of the above are warranted.

Contributed by

Florida State

University

SOLUTIONS FOR COLLEGE LEVEL SKILLS IN COMPUTATION FORM A

1. To add fractions, first convert both fractions to a common denominator.

   $\frac{3}{4} \times \frac{3}{3} = \frac{9}{12}$ and $\frac{5}{6} \times \frac{2}{2} = \frac{10}{12}$. $\frac{9}{12} + \frac{10}{12} = \frac{19}{12} = 1\frac{7}{12}$ Answer [c]

   (a) is wrong because the denominators were added. Answer (b) is equal to a. Answer (d) has the correct denominator but wrong numerator. (e) added the denominators.

2. $8\frac{7}{8} - 1\frac{1}{4} = 8\frac{7}{8} - 1\frac{2}{8} = 7\frac{5}{8}$ Answer [a]

   Answer (b) subtracted the numerators without finding a common denominator. (c) left off the 7. (d) subtracted the denominators. (e) used the wrong denominator.

3. Before multiplying, change the mixed number to an improper fraction.

   $\frac{3}{8} \times 1\frac{1}{3} = \frac{3}{8} \times \frac{4}{3} = \frac{12}{24} = \frac{1}{2}$ Answer [a]

   Answer (b) was obtained by failing to use an improper fraction for $1\frac{1}{3}$.

   Answer (c) inverted the correct answer. (d) has a arithmetic error. (e) is equal to answer a but not reduced. (f) was obtained by inverting the fraction $\frac{4}{3}$ before multiplying.

4. To divide fractions invert the second fraction and multiply.

   $3\frac{1}{2} \div \frac{1}{2} = \frac{7}{2} \times \frac{2}{1} = \frac{14}{2} = 7$ Answer [b]

   (a) failed to invert $\frac{1}{2}$ before multiplying. (c) is the reciprocal of b. (d) eliminated the fractions and left the 3. (f) resulted from inverting both fractions before multiplying.

5. To add decimal numerals write as shown; keep the decimal points in a vertical column.

   ```
     .595
   + .630
   ------
   1.225
   ```

   Answers a and e misplace the decimal. (c) resulted because numbers were aligned on the right and (d) is another version of c with the decimal moved. Answer [b]

6. To subtract decimal numerals write in vertical fashion with the decimal points in a column. Attach zeros to fill in columns as shown below.

   ```
    310.500
   -  2.025
   --------
    308.475
   ```

   Answers a, b, and e resulted from aligning the numbers on the right. (c) failed to borrow correctly from the .5. Answer [d]

7. To multiply decimal numerals, multiply as whole numbers are multiplied. The number of digits placed right of the decimal in the answer equals the total number of digits right of the decimals in the two multipliers.

```
  1 0.6
x   .0 3
-------
 .3 1 8
```

The other answers resulted from miscounting the digits right of the decimal points in the multipliers.   Answer [c]

8. If there is a decimal point in the divisor of a division problem, move both decimal points to the right to create a whole number divisor as shown below.

```
        5.3
.05. ) 2.6.5
        2 5
        ---
        1 5
        1 5
        ---
          0
```

The other answers resulted from misplacing the decimal point. Notice that .05, the divisor, is placed outside the division sign.

Answer [b]

9. [b] is correct because 34.8 cm is closer to 35 cm than 34 cm. The rule for rounding off is: If the digit right of the desired place is 5 or greater, add one to the digit in the place and drop the other digits on the right. If the digit on the right is less than 5, drop the digits on the right and leave the digit in the desired place as it was.   Answer [b]

10. [a] is correct because the digit 2 is right of the digit 4 (in the hundreds place). 7425 is closer to 74-hundred than 75-hundred.   Answer [a]

11. Answer [d] is correct because the measurement is closer to 1 1/2 than it is to 1 1/4. (b) is wrong because it is not to the nearest 1/4 inch. (c) is too far from the end of the measure.   Answer [d]

12. To find the volume of a room, multiply the length by the width by the height. 40 x 25 x 3 = 3,000 cubic meters, answer [a] Answer c is in wrong units.   Answer [a]

13. To find the surface area of the solid: 1) find the area of each face (there are 6 altogether) and 2) add them together.

```
face 1) 8 x 2 =  16
face 2) 8 x 10 = 80
face 3) 2 x 10 = 20
---------------------
total          116
116 x 2 = 232 square inches,
```

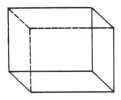

Answer [d]

14. To find the circumference of the circle use the steps below.
$C = \pi D = \pi 6 = 6\pi$, Answer [a] Answers b and c misused the formula and d found the area of the circle instead of the circumference. Answer [a]

15. There are 1,000 cubic centimeters (cc.) in 1 liter.
1.75 liters = 1,750 cu. cm.   Answer [d]

16. The correct answer is [c] as only like terms may be combined. The other answers either added or multiplied incorrectly.   Answer [c]

17. To multiply square roots, multiply the numbers under the radical signs and simplify as shown.
$\sqrt{3} \times \sqrt{6} = \sqrt{18} = \sqrt{9} \times \sqrt{2} = 3\sqrt{2}$,
Answer b is not simplified. Answers c, d, and e have misinterpreted the problem.   Answer [a]

18. To subtract radicals, simplify first and then combine like terms as shown.
$\sqrt{50} - \sqrt{18} = \sqrt{25}\sqrt{2} - \sqrt{9}\sqrt{2} = 5\sqrt{2} - 3\sqrt{2} = 2\sqrt{2}$,
Answer b was obtained by subtracting before simplifying.   Answer [a]

19. To divide by a radical use the steps below to eliminate the radical from the denominator.
$$\frac{15}{3\sqrt{2}} = \frac{15}{3\sqrt{2}} \times \frac{\sqrt{2}}{\sqrt{2}} = \frac{15\sqrt{2}}{3\sqrt{4}} = \frac{5\sqrt{2}}{2}$$ Answer [b]

20. In expressions similar to problems 20, 21, and 22, complete the multiplication and division first from left to right and then complete the addition and subtraction from left to right as shown:
$2 \times 3 + 8 \div 2 = 6 + 4 = 10$,
Answer a is the result of added before dividing. (c) was done from right to left.   Answer [b]

21. $-14t - 2t \times 3 + 21t^2 \div 7 \times 3$
$-14t - 6t + 3t^2 \times 3$ Answer [a]
$-14t - 6t + 9t^2$
$-20t + 9t^2$.   The other answers are the result of adding or subtracting before multiplication or division was done.

22. $6t - (5t) \times (2) + 3t = 6t - 10t + 3t = -4t + 3t = -t$,   Answer [b]
Answer (a) subtracted before multiplying. (c) has the wrong sign.

23. To complete the division divide 2.4 by 1.2 to obtain 2. Then division of 10^3 by 10^{-2} is done by changing the sign of the denominator exponent, -2, and adding to the numerator exponent 3 to obtain 10^5.
Answer (b) added the exponents without changing the sign. (c) changed the wrong sign.   Answer [a]

24. To multiply, write each numeral in scientific notation, multiply, and simplify as shown.
$.0004 \times 170{,}000 = (4 \times 10^{-4}) \times (1.7 \times 10^{5}) = 6.8 \times 10^{1}$,   Answer [a]

25. Equations and inequalities are solved or simplified by adding opposites to eliminate terms that are added or subtracted and then multiplying by reciprocals as shown in the following steps. **Note:** When multiplying both sides of an equality by a negative number, the sign of the inequality will reverse. For example, $>$ will reverse to $<$.

$$3x - 1 \geq 5x + 5$$
$$\underline{+ 1 + 1}$$
$$3x \geq 5x + 6$$
$$\underline{-5x -5x}$$
$$-2x \geq 6$$
$$-\tfrac{1}{2}(-2x) \leq -\tfrac{1}{2}(6) \quad \text{Note: } \geq \text{ changed to } \leq.$$
$$x \leq -3 \text{Answer [c]}$$

Answer a did not reverse $\geq$.

26. $5x - 2 = 3x + 6$
$2x = 8$ and $x = 4$ Answer [a]

27. Multiply both portions of the equation by 3/2 to obtain $x = 45/2$ or
22 1/2,   Answer [d]

28. $3(x + 2) = 2[x - (1 - x)]$ Answers b, c, and d are the result of incor-
$3x + 6 = 2[x - 1 + x]$ rect removal of the parentheses. **Note** the
$3x + 6 = 2x - 2 + 2x$ fact that $-(1 - x) = -1 + x$.
$3x + 6 = 4x - 2$
$8 = x$ Answer [a]

29. To find y in the expression when $x = 0$ replace x with 0 in the equation as shown below.
$y = x^{2} + 2x - 3 = 0^{2} + 2(0) - 3 = 0 + 0 - 3 = -3$ Answer [b]
Answer a is the result of treating 0 like a 1. (c) has the sign left off and (d) could result from treating 0 like a 1 and ignoring the sign of -3.

30. Replace b with -1 and simplify. $a = (b - 2)^{2} = (-1 - 2)^{2} = (-3)^{2} = 9$,
Answer a is the result of adding -1 and -2 incorrectly.
(d) resulted from failing to multiply -3 by itself.   Answer [c]

31. To find the Celcius temperature, replace F with 86 in the formula and simplify as shown below.
$C = \tfrac{5}{9}(F - 32) = \tfrac{5}{9}(86 - 32) = \tfrac{5}{9}(54) = 30°$, Answer a is the result of multiplying 86 by 5/9 before subtracting 32. **Note:** The operation enclosed in the parentheses is to be completed first.   Answer [b]

32. In this formula, multiplication should be accomplished first before addition is completed. $F = \frac{9}{5}C + 32 = \frac{9}{5}(35) + 32 = 9(7) + 32 = 63 + 32 = 95°$.

    Answer a is the result of adding first instead of multiplying

    Answer [c]

33. To find the interest replace P with 6,000, R with .14, and T with 2 in the formula.
    $I = PRT = 6,000 \times .14 \times 2 = 12,000 \times .14 = \$1,680$ Answer [b]

34. To find the difference in the sales, find the sales for October and subtract the sales for January. Since the figures on the scale on the left represent $1,000 of dollars, the sales for October is $60,000 and $40,000 for January to give a difference of $20,000. The other answers are the result of misreading the line graph.   Answer [c]

35. The top of the bar representing "Thursday" is across from 65°.   Answer [d]
    The other answers are the temperatures of the other days shown.

36. To find the percent add the hours in English and natural science and divide by the total number of hours required. Then convert the decimal to percent. $(9 + 10) \div 36 = 19/36$ or approximately .527 or 52.7%.

    Answer [e]
    (f) is the result of dividing 10 by 36. (c) is the result of dividing 9 by 36. (b) is the result of dividing 9 by 19. (a) and (c) are arithmetic errors.

37. To find the mean, add the items and divide by the total number of items.
    $$\frac{5 + 6 + 5 + 3 + 6 + 7 + 6 + 2}{8} = \frac{40}{8} = 5,$$
    Answer [b]
    (c) is the median of the data but not the mean.

38. There are an even number of items (10) in the list; the median is the item half-way between the two items in the middle of the distribution when placed in sequence as shown below.
    3   5   5   6   <u>6   6</u>   8   9   10   12
    Since the middle pair of items are both 6's, the median is 6.   Answer [a]
    If one had been 5 and the other 6 the median would have been 5.5, the average of 5 and 6.
    If the number of items is odd, the median is the middle item.

39. The mode of a set of data is the item that occurs most often. 21 appears four times in the list and this makes 21 the mode of the data.
    (e) is the median.
    Answer [a]

40. The simple events in an experiment is <u>a set</u> containing all the events possible in the experiments. There should four ordered pairs in the event space; 5 and 9 should be the first components and 2 and 6 the second components. **Answer [b]**

41. (1) is true because every element is in U. (2) is false; some elements of A and B are in set C. (3) is false because some elements of U are not in B. **Answer [a]**

42. (1) is true because the word "and" means the elements must be in both A and C. (2) is true as U contains all the elements. (3) is false because some elements are in U that are not in C. **Answer [d]**

43. 2^3 means 2 x 2 x 2 and 5^2 means 5 x 5. **Answer [d]**
(a) is the result of adding instead of multiplying. (b) and (c) have combined unlike bases. (e), (f), and (g) have violated other rules of exponents.

44. To find the place value count from the decimal point. 5 is in the second place to the right of the decimal point (hundredths). **Answer [b]**
(a) would be correct for the digit 0, (c) is correct for the digit 6 three places right of the point and (d) for the 6 left of the decimal which is in the ones place.

45. To find the base-ten equivalent of a numeral in another base, expand the numeral using the steps below.
224 (base 5) = $2 \times 5^2 + 2 \times 5^1 + 4 \times 5^0$ = 2 x 25 + 10 + 4 = 64 (base ten)
The other answers are the result of a misuse of an expansion. **Answer [d]**

46. To convert a decimal numeral to a percent, the decimal point should be moved two places to the right. Consequently, .2 = 20% **Answer [c]**
The other answers are a result of misplacing the decimal point.

47. To change a percent to a decimal, move the decimal point two places to the left. Consequently, 150% = 150.% = 1.5 **Answer [c]**
Misplacing the decimal generated the other answers.

48. To convert 13/25 to a percent, divide 13 by 25 to obtain .52 or 52%. All the other answers have misplaced decimals. **Answer [d]**

49. To compare two fractions, write them using a common denominator as shown below. $\frac{3}{4} = \frac{27}{36}$ and $\frac{8}{9} = \frac{32}{36}$. Consequently $\frac{3}{4} < \frac{8}{9}$. **Answer [a]**

50.   Answer [b]

51. $1.2\overline{5}$ = 1.2555 . . . and $\underline{1.\overline{25}}$ = 1.25252525 . . ..
      1.25 is greater than 1.25 because there is a 5 in the
      thousandths place of 1.2555 . . . and only a 2 in the corresponding
      place of 1.252525 . . ..   Answer [b]

52.   To aid in comparing the numerals, 1/5 can be converted to a decimal by
      dividing 1 by 5 to obtain .20.   Answer [b]

53.   6.32 = 6.320 and is therefore greater than 6.032.   Answer [b]
      Note: The zero in 6.032 has pushed the 2 in the hundredths place in
      6.32 to the thousandths place in 6.032, a much smaller place value.

54.   (1) is false because the two lines are intersecting. (2) and (3) are true.
                                                                          Answer [f]

55.   (1) is false because AB is perpendicular to BC and only one line through
      A can be perpendicular to BC. (2) is true because each exterior angle
      of a triangle has a measure equal to the sum of the measures of its two
      remote interior angles. (3) is true because the sum of the measures of
      a triangle's interior angles is always 180°. (4) is true because two
      adjacent angles whose non-common rays form a line are supplementary
      angles.   Answer [f]

56.   1 is true as vertical angles are congruent (equal measure). 2 is false
      as 5 and 6 are supplementary. 3 is also false as the two angles add up
      to 180° (are supplementary) and not complementary (add up to 90°).
                                                                          Answer [a]

57.   All four figures are quadrilaterals. The rhombus and parallelogram
      have opposites sides which are parallel, but their diagonals will not be
      congruent unless the figures are rectangles. A trapezoid is only re-
      quired to have one pair of parallel sides and its diagonals are not
      necessarily congruent.   Answer [d]

58.   It is possible to have a right isosceles triangle which is a right
      triangle with two sides of equal length. It is possible to have an
      isosceles acute triangle which is a triangle with two equal sides and
      all angles less than 90°. It is impossible to have a right obtuse tri-
      angle which is a triangle with an angle greater than 90° and also a right
      angle. It is impossible to have a right equilateral triangle because
      when all three sides have the same length then all three angles must
      have the same measure (60°).   Answer [g]

59. The angle shown in b is the only one less than 90° which is the definition of an acute angle.   Answer [b]

60. Only 1 and 2 show figures with opposite sides parallel and at least one 90° angle. Correct answer [f]

61. (2) is false because the two angles are in the same triangle and are not forced to be congruent. (1) is false for the same reason. (3) is true because the triangles are similar; DE corresponds to AC and BE corresponds to BC on the larger triangle. (4) is false because corresponding segments were not used in the proportion.   Answer [3]

62. Two triangles are similar when they have equal measures for their three angles or when their corresponding sides are proportional. The triangles in 1 have corresponding angles equal as do the triangles in 3; each has a 90° angle and vertical angles are equal.   Answer [e]

63. Statement (1) is true as the corresponding sides of similar triangles are proportional. (2) is false as DE should measure 12 because the ratio of the sides is 3 to 1. (3) is true as angle W is vertical to Z.   Answer [e]

64. The object is a line segment.   Answer [a]

65. Areas are measured in square units.   Answer [b]

66. Volume is measured in cubic units.   Answer [c]

67. The parentheses enclose different terms on each side of the statement and the order remained the same. The properties below are useful for passing the CLAST and should be memorized.   Answer [b]

$$a + b = b + a \quad \text{and} \quad ab = ba \qquad \text{Commutative}$$
$$(a + b) + c = a + (b + c) \quad \text{and} \quad (ab)c = a(bc) \qquad \text{Associative}$$
$$a(b + c) = ab + ac \qquad \text{Distributive}$$
$$a + 0 = a \quad \text{and} \quad 1a = a \qquad \text{Identity Elements}$$

68. The multiplication has been distributed over the addition problem $a + b$.
Answer [e]

69. The order of a and b has been reversed on the right side of the equation.
Answer [b]

70. $5(7) + 5(a) = 5(7 + a)$ by the distributive property.   Answer [e]

71. To answer the question replace the letter with -3 in each statement.
1. $|x-1| = 4$; $|-3-1| = |-4| = 4$; true
2. $(x + 4)(x + 2) \leq -1$; $(-3 + 4)(-3 + 2) \leq -1$; $1 \cdot -1 \leq -1$, true
3. $6x \leq x + 3$; $6(-3) \leq -3 + 3$; $-18 \leq 0$, true   Answer [g]

145

72. To answer the question replace x with –1 in each statement.

1. $\frac{-1}{3} x = \frac{1}{3}$; $\frac{-1}{3} (-1) = \frac{1}{3}$, true

2. $(3x + 1)(x - 1) < 0$; $[3(-1)+ 1](-1 - 1) < 0$; $(-3 + 1)(-2) < 0$, $-2(-2) < 0$, false   Answer [a]

3. (c) will be false because –1 times –3/5 will produce a positive number.

73. The fraction 3/8 compares "A" students to total students and the other fraction in the proportion must make the same comparison.   Answer [c]

74. Distance equals rate times time. As a result, there is an inverse proportion between the ratio of the times and the ratio of the rates. Only (d) reflects this relationship. Note that (a) is equivalent to (c).   Answer [d]

75. Figure a is incorrect because it shows y < 0. Figure b is incorrect because it shows x < 0. Figure c is incorrect because it shows y < 0. Figure d shows x ≥ 0, y ≥ 0 and y ≤ 2.   Answer [d]

76. Only answer [c] is correct as the shaded area shows x values greater than or equal to zero **and** less than or equal to 2. It also shows that y can take on any value. (a) would show a horizontal area across the graph. (b) has no solutions. (d) includes all the points of the plane because of the use of the word or.   Answer [c]

77. (a) shows the graph of x + y = 2. (b) is the graph of y = |x| + 2. (c) is the correct answer; (2,0),(1,1),(0,2) and (–1,–1) are some of the solutions for |x| + |y| = 2. Figure (d) is the graph of |x| – |y| = 2. To confirm the answers try some ordered pairs in each equation to find the ones that are solutions.   Answer [c]

78. Statement 1 is true as most of the data lies near the mean as shown by the graph on the right. 2 is also true as the normal curve is symmetric about the mean. 3 is false as only about 5% of the data lies more than 2 standard deviations from the mean.

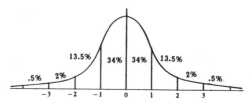

    Answer [d]

79. To answer this question, the data in each row can be tested to find the row that conforms the closest to the percents given. In this particular situation the fact that the number of trucks and compacts is the same quickly eliminates samples (a) and (d). Figuring percents for the numbers in (c) shows sizable differences, but figuring percents for the numbers in (b) show only slight differences.   Answer [b]

80. The probability that the first ball drawn is red is $\frac{3}{9}$ because there are three red balls and 9 balls altogether in the sample space. After the red ball is drawn there are 2 red balls and 8 balls left to give a probability of $\frac{2}{8}$. The probability that both balls drawn are red is $\frac{3}{9}$ x $\frac{2}{8}$ (c) assumes that the balls are replaced as they are drawn.   Answer [e]

81. This question can be solved two ways. One way is to add the probability of obtaining two heads, the probability of obtaining a head and then a tail, and the probability of obtaining a tail and then a head. The second and easier method is to subtract the probability of obtaining two tails from 1; P(A) = 1 - P(not A) is a valuable rule of probability. The probability of obtaining two heads is 1/4 so the probability of obtaining two heads or one head and one tail is 1 - 1/4 = 3/4. Answer (a) means that the event will always happen. Answer (e) means that the event will never happen.   Answer [b]

82. The sentence "Sam is a barber and George is a butcher" is in the form "p and q" which has the negation "not p or not q". Only sentence [b] has that form. None of the rest have the same truth value; a fact which can be checked with a truth table.   Answer [b]

83. The sentence "Bob wants to both go to the beach and go to a movie" is in the form "p and q" which has the negation "not p or not q" or "if p then not q". Use of this second negation form gives the correct result.   Answer [b]

84. "not both p and q" is equivalent to "not p or not q" (b) and "if p then not q" (c) and "if q the not p" (d). Consequently the answer not logically equivalent to the given statement is [a].

85. The given sentence is an implication of the form $p \longrightarrow q$ and is equivalent to its contrapositive $\sim q \longrightarrow \sim p$.   Answer [c]

86. The negation of "All p are q" is "some p are not q".   Answer [a]

87. An implication (p $\longrightarrow$ q) is changed to its converse (q $\longrightarrow$ p) by
swapping the hypothesis with the conclusion.　　Answer [d]
Note: The other forms of the implication above which may be needed
for other CLAST questions are:
the inverse: ~p $\longrightarrow$ ~q　　　　the contrapositive: ~q $\longrightarrow$ ~p

88. All of the applicants lack at least one of the qualifications.　　Answer [e]

89. (a) and (b) cannot be deduced.　(d) is true, but not directly deduced.
　　　　　　　　　　　　　　　　　　　　　　Answer [c]

90. (1) is valid.　(2) is not valid.　(3) is valid. (4) is invalid.　　Answer [2,4]

91. (1) uses a word two ways and is fallacious.　(3) is a fallacy because Dr.
Good may have no expertise in politics.　　Answer [b]

92. (1) and (2) are fallacies because they assume, incorrectly, that "if p then q"
is equivalent to "if q then p".　(3) is a fallacy because it assumes the whole
has the same property as the part.　　Answer [g]

93. (1) is a fallacy because it assumes, incorrectly, that "if not p then not q" is
equivalent to "if p then q".　(3) is a fallacy because an individual's reply to
a self-incriminating question may not divulge the full truth.
　　　　　　　　　　　　　　　　　　　　　　Answer [b]

94. A proof by contradiction will use given facts to show that the negation
of the statement to be proved is false.　In (2) the argument contradicts
"he did buy the hardware."　(1) and (4) are examples of chains of impl-
cations.　(3) is valid because both parts of an "and" statement must be
true.　　Answer [b]

95. The robot is repeating the task hundreds of times a day.　The important
capability is repetition.　　Answer [b]

96. Answers a, c, and d essentially require the computer to do one task.
Many different decisions based on current data are required to run a
farm.　　Answer [b]

97. Bob only had to prepare and input the data.　The other tasks were either
already done by the computer or not required.　　Answer [c]

98. Answer [a, d]

99. In each pair, the second component is three times smaller than the first
component.　To find the second component multiply by 1/3.　　Answer [d]

100. In the progression, each term is multiplied by $-\frac{1}{2}$ to obtain the next term. $(\frac{3}{8})(-\frac{1}{2}) = -\frac{3}{16}$.   Answer [b]

101. See the answer for problem 67 for examples of the properties.   Answer [c]

102. [a]

103. The area of one of the triangles is $\frac{1}{2}$bh. Therefore the formula
     for the total area is (a).   Answer [a]

104. The surface area of one side of the cube is s^2 and the exposed surface
     area of the cube is $5s^2$. The area of one face of the pyramid is $\frac{1}{2}$sh.
     Therefore the total area is given by (b).   Answer [b]

105. (c) is the only correct formula as it is the only one to subtract 2 from
     the number of sides before multiplying by 180°.   Answer [c]

106. The first exponent plus two times the second exponent gives the third
     exponent in each example.   Answer [c]

107. The sum of the first two exponents divided by the third exponent give
     the fourth exponent in each example.   Answer [b]

108. Two was subtracted from each component in the first statement to obtain
     the second statement. This is allowed by the additive property of inequal-
     ities. **Note:** Inequalities are solved with steps similar to equations
     with the exception of property (d).   Answer [a]

109. Both sides of the first inequality were multiplied by $-1/2$ to obtain
     the second inequality. This is an example of property (d).   Answer [d]

110. (a) (b), and (d) do not match the given information. (d) gives the number
     of outcomes when flipped a coin (2 sides) n times.   Answer [c]

111. The number of ways are:
        3 objects = 3,   4 objects = 6,   5 objects = 10
     The previous number of objects is added to the number of ways. Therefore
        6 objects = 5+10=15,   7 objects = 6+15=21   Answer [c]

112. Each argument consists of an "or" statement and the negation of one of
     the subsentences of the statement forces the other portion to be true. (b)
     and (d) are invalid and (c) is valid because both parts of an "and" sen-
     tence must be true.   Answer [a]

113. The two statements given have the form of generalization 1.   Answer [1]

114. If p represents "dogs are rabid" then rule 4 shows that the two statements are equivalent.   Answer [4]

115. 30% of $320 = .30 x $320 = $96 and $320 - $96 = $224   Answer [a]
30% of $184 = .30 x $184 = $55.20 and $55.20 + $184 = $239.20

116. Both 7 and 21 give a remainder of 3 when divided into 66 and a remainder
of 2 when divided into 23.   Answer [a]

117. The number 18 and 48 are numbers that leave a remainder of 3 when
divided by 5 and are also evenly divisible by 2 and 6.   Answer [b]

118. To find the total cost the following steps are used.
roof area = 40 x 30 = 1200 sq. ft.
porch area = 9 x 9 =   81 sq. ft.
Total area   = 1281 sq. ft.
1281 $\div$ 100 = 12.81 or 13 bundles of roofing at $70 = $910
$910 + $275 = $1,185 total cost, Answer a is the sum of $100 and $275.
(b) only allows for 12 bundles of roofing and d does not include the
roofing cost at all.   Answer [c]

119. The path of the ship forms the
hypotenuse (c) of a right triangle
as shown in the figure with legs
(a,b) of 16 and 12. The Pythagorean
Theorem gives:
$a^2 + b^2 = c^2$
$(16)^2 + (12)^2 = c^2$
256   + 144 = c^2 and c^2 = 400. Therefore c = 20 miles
Answer b added the two legs. The other answers are the
result of other misunderstandings.   Answer [a]

120. To find the total number of bass in the lake a proportion can be used
with each side using the number of tagged bass in the numerator and the
total number of bass in the denominator.
$$\frac{\text{tagged bass}}{\text{total no.}} \quad \frac{50}{x} = \frac{40}{400} \quad 40x = 50(400) \text{ and } x = 500 \text{ bass} \quad \text{Answer [c]}$$

121. The value of the equipment after four years is found by finding the average depreciation per year and subtracting four times that amount from
the original cost as shown below.
$3,000 - $200 = $2,800 and $2,800 $\div$ 10 = $280 depreciation per year.
Loss of value in four years = 4 x $280 = $1,120
Value after four years = $3,000 - $1,120 = $1,880   Answer [c]

122. Using (r) for speed and (d) for length of skid marks, the fact that
d varies directly as r^2 gives the equation $d = kr^2$ where k is
a constant. Substituting $d = 40$ and $r = 30$, the equation can be solved
for k.

$$d = kr^2 \text{ becomes } 40 = k \cdot 30^2 \text{ or } k = \frac{4}{90}$$

Now the value for k can be used with the fact that $d = 140$ to find r.

$$140 = r^2(\frac{4}{90}) \text{ gives } \frac{90}{4}(140) = r^2$$

$3150 = r^2$ and r is approximately 56.1 mph
If r and d had varied indirectly, the formula would be $r^2d = k$. Answer [b]

123. Let x represent the number. Then twice the number is 2x and 4 more than
twice the number is $4 + 2x$. The sum of the number, x, and $4 + 2x$ is
found in (d).   Answer [d]

124. If x is replaced by 1, (a) is true. (b) and (c) are easy to prove true
also. No number divided into 9 will ever give 0.   Answer [d]

125. A score of 54 is one standard deviation below the mean of 60. The percent
of the area under the normal curve between the mean and one standard deviation below the mean is about .341 or 34%. Therefore, the percent of the
area under the curve that is less than one standard deviation below the mean
is 50% - 34% = 16% which means that about 16% of the applicants will
be refused admission to the college. (a) is the result of failing to subtract
34% from 50%. (c) is the percent of the area above one standard deviation
below the mean and (d) is the percent of area within one standard deviation
above or below the mean.   Answer [b]

126. The probability of drawing two women from the group is $\frac{25}{50}$ x $\frac{24}{49}$.
Since the probability of drawing two men is the same as for drawing the
women, the answer is [b].   Answer [b]

127. The odds of 5:8 means that in 5 efforts she gets the job and in 8 efforts
she does not. Therefore there are 13 possibilities in all. As a result,
the probability of **not** obtaining the job is 8/13.   Answer [d]

128. The "and" sentence indicates that you are a lawyer and the first sentence
states that if you are a lawyer, you will be successful.   Answer [a]

129. A valid conclusion must follow logically from the premises. (a) is not
a valid conclusion because many people other than lawyers go to the opera
Bill could be a lawyer so (b) is not a valid conclusion. (c) is not
a valid conclusion because some dumb people may like opera too. (d) isn't
valid either as the intelligent people who like opera are not forced to
be lawyers by these premises.   Answer [e]

The answers for Sample Test B are below. They are less complete than the answers given for Sample Test A. If further explanation is needed, find a matching problem from Sample Test A (similar problems have approximately the same number in the two sample tests).

SOLUTIONS FOR COLLEGE LEVEL SKILLS IN COMPUTATION   FORM B

1. $\frac{2}{3} \times \frac{2}{2} + \frac{1}{2} \times \frac{3}{3} = \frac{4}{6} + \frac{3}{6} = \frac{7}{6} = 1\frac{1}{6}$ Answer [a]

2. $7\frac{5}{6} - \frac{1}{3} = 7\frac{5}{6} - \frac{2}{6} = 7\frac{3}{6} = 7\frac{1}{2}$ Answer [b]

3. $\frac{3}{4} \times 1\frac{1}{5} = \frac{3}{4} \times \frac{6}{5} = \frac{3}{\cancel{4}_2} \times \frac{\cancel{6}^3}{5} = \frac{9}{10}$ Answer [d]

4. $4\frac{2}{3} \div \frac{1}{3} = \frac{14}{3} \div \frac{1}{3} = \frac{14}{\cancel{3}_1} \times \frac{\cancel{3}^1}{1} = 14$ Answer [d]

5.
```
    .623
 + 4.420
   5.043
```
Answer [a]

6.
```
  106.20
 - 17.08
   89.12
```
Answer [b]

7.
```
   1 9.6
 x   2.5
     9 8 0
   3 9 2
   4 9.0 0
```
Answer [a]

8.
```
          .6 2
 .4.)0.2.4 8
      2 4
        0 8
          8
          0
```
Answer [d]

9. [a]   10. [b]   11. [b]

12. 25 x 30 = 750 and 750 x 8 = 6,000 cubic feet.   Answer [b]

13.
```
 9 x  4 =  36
 9 x 12 = 108
 4 x 12 =  48
          192 x 2 = 384 square centimeters.
```
Answer [c]

14. $A = \pi r^2 = \pi(3)^2 = 9\pi$ Answer [d]

15. 1 liter equals 1,000 milliliters. Thus, 1,275 ml = 1.275 liters.   Answer [b]

16. [a]

17. $\sqrt{2} \times \sqrt{12} = \sqrt{24} = \sqrt{4} \times \sqrt{6} = 2\sqrt{6}$ Answer [b]

18. $\sqrt{45} - \sqrt{80} = \sqrt{9}\sqrt{5} - \sqrt{16}\sqrt{5} = 3\sqrt{5} - 4\sqrt{5} = -\sqrt{5}$ Answer [d]

19. $\dfrac{\cancel{12}^3}{\cancel{4}_1 \sqrt{3}} \times \dfrac{\sqrt{3}}{\sqrt{3}} = \dfrac{3\sqrt{3}}{\sqrt{9}} = \dfrac{3\sqrt{3}}{3} = \sqrt{3}$ Answer [d]

20. $\dfrac{1}{2} - 8(\dfrac{1}{4} + 1) = \dfrac{1}{2} - 8(\dfrac{5}{4}) = \dfrac{1}{2} - 10 = \dfrac{1}{2} - \dfrac{20}{2} = -\dfrac{19}{2} = -9\dfrac{1}{2}$ Answer [c]

21. $3a^2 \div a + 2a \times 2 - 5a$
    $3a \quad + \quad 4a \quad - \quad 5a \quad = \quad 2a$ Answer [a]

22. $8t - 3 \times 2t + 5t = 8t - 6t + 5t = 7t$ Answer [d]

23. $\dfrac{5.6}{1.4} = 4$ and $\dfrac{10^{-3}}{10^{-2}} = 10^{-1}$ Answer [b]

24. To add the numerals, first write 1.2×10^4 as 12×10^3 using the following steps.
$2.5 \times 10^3 + 1.2 \times 10^4 = 2.5 \times 10^3 + 1.2 \times 10^1 \times 10^3 = 2.5 \times 10^3 + 12 \times 10^3$
$= 14.5 \times 10^3 = 1.45 \times 10^1 \times 10^3 = 1.45 \times 10^4$ Answer [c]

25. $\quad\quad\quad -2x - 3 \leq 3x + 7$
$\quad\quad\quad\quad\quad - 3 \leq 5x + 7$
$\quad\quad\quad\quad -10 \leq 5x$ and $x \geq -2$ Answer [c]

26. $\quad\quad\quad 7x + 3 = 9x - 5$
$\quad\quad\quad -2x + 3 = -5$
$\quad\quad\quad\quad\quad -2x = -8$
$\quad\quad\quad\quad\quad\quad x = 4$ Answer [d]

27. $\quad\quad\quad\quad -\dfrac{3}{4}x = 16$

$\quad -\dfrac{4}{3}(-\dfrac{3}{4})x = (16)-\dfrac{4}{3}$

$\quad\quad\quad\quad\quad x = -\dfrac{64}{3} = -21\dfrac{1}{3}$ Answer [a]

Answers Test B

28.
$$5[x - (2x - 3)] = 2(x - 3)$$
$$5[x - 2x + 3] = 2x - 6$$
$$5[-x + 3] = 2x - 6$$
$$-5x + 15 = 2x - 6$$
$$-7x = -21 \text{ and } x = 3$$
Answer [b]

29. When $x = 0$, $y = (x - 6)^2 = (0 - 6)^2 = (-6)^2 = 36$ Answer [d]

30. When $b = -2$, $a = b^2 - 2b - 3 = (-2)^2 - 2(-2) - 3 = 4 + 4 - 3 = 5$
Answer [d]

31. When $F = 68°$, $C = \frac{5}{9}(F - 32) = \frac{5}{9}(68 - 32) = \frac{5}{9}(36) = 20°$ Answer [c]

32. When $C = 30°$, $F = \frac{9}{5}(30) + 32 = \frac{9}{\cancel{5}_1}(\cancel{30})^6 + 32 = 54 + 32 = 86°$
Answer [a]

33. When $C = \$12$ and $M = 40\%$, $P = C + MC = 12 + .40(12)$
$$= 12 + 4.80 = \$16.80$$ Answer [d]

34. $60 - 40 = 20$ Answer [e]

35. [d]   36. [e]

37. The average (sum of the numbers divided by the number of numbers) is 7.
Answer [c]

38. 1 3 4 5 <u>5 6</u> 6 6 9 10   The median is between the middle pair of items, 5
and 6. $\frac{5 + 6}{2} = \frac{11}{2} = 5.5$ Answer [c]

39. 10 11 12 12 <u>13 13 13</u> 15 15 17   The number 13 appears the most number
of times and is therefore the mode.   Answer [c]

40. [a]   41. [e]   42. [b]   43. [d]   44. [a]   45. [c]

46. 133 (base-five) $= 1 \times 5^2 + 3 \times 5^1 + 3 = 25 + 15 + 3 = 43$ Answer [b]

47. [b]   48. [b]

49. $9 \div 16 = 0.5625$ which is approximately 56.3%   Answer [d]

50. Both fractions reduce to $-\frac{2}{3}$.   Answer [c]

51. $(\frac{4}{3})^2 = \frac{16}{9} = 1\frac{7}{9} > \frac{4}{3}$ Answer [b]

52. $10.\overline{345} = 10.345345345...$ and $10.3\overline{45} = 10.3454545...$ Answer [a]

53. $1/3 = .333...$ which is greater than -0.25 Answer [a]

54. 8.052 is less than 8.100 because 52-thousandths is less than 100-thousandths.
          Answer [a]

55. [c]

56. Statement 2 is true because the triangle has two 60° angles and this forces angle K to also be 60°. Statement 3 is true because when parallel lines are cut by a transversal, the interior angles on the same side of the transversal are supplementary.   Answer [f]

57. Angles F is a corresponding angle to the 60° angle so 1 is true. Angle J is supplemental to angle K and angle A is congruent to angle J. Consequently, angle A is supplemental to angle K. Angles A and J are congruent and corresponding.   Answer [e]

58. [d]

59. Squares and rectangles both must have 90° angles and congruent diagonals. Trapezoids need only one pair of parallel sides. Only rhombii meet all the given conditions.   Answer [b]

60. An obtuse angle measures more than 90° and less than 180°.   Answer [a]

61. A trapezoid is a quadrilateral with at least one pair of parallel sides Therefore squares, rectangles and parallelograms are also trapezoids because they all have at least one pair of parallel sides.   Answer [h]

62. Statement 2 is false because BE is not a side of either triangle. If BC was used instead of BE, 2 would be true.   Answer [a]

63. The pair of triangles in 1 are similar; they have a pair of congruent (vertical) angles and those angles are between two pairs of sides in equal ratios. The pair of triangles in 2 are both 30°, 60°, 90° triangles and therefore similar.   Answer [g]

64. Statement (2) is true as the corresponding sides of the two triangles are in a 2/1 ratio. Since CD measures 6 units, BC must measure 3 units to be in a 2/1 ratio. (1) is false because ED does not correspond to AC. (3) is false because angle B corresponds to angle D not angle E.

Answer [b]

65. Length requires a linear measure. Answer [a]

66. Area requires a square measure. Answer [b]

67. Volume requires cubic measure. Answer [c]

68. [g]

69. The order of the expressions on the right side of the equation has been reversed; therefore, it is an example of the commutative law. Answer [d]

70. The statements and the illustrated laws are as follows:
    (a) – associative law of multiplication.
    (b) – commutative laws of multiplication and addition.
    (c) – commutative law of multiplication.
    (d) – distributive law of multiplication over addition.
    (f) – not a true statement. Answer [e]

71. By the associative law of addition, answer b is equivalent to the given statement. Answer [b]

72. When $x = -1$ statement 1 is true, because $(-1 - 1)(-1 - 2) \geq 3$
    Statement 2 is false because $|-1-1| = |-2| = + 2$; false. Answer [e]
    Statement 3 is true because $3(-1) < 2(-1) + 1$ is $-3 < -1$; true.
    Statement 4 is true because $(-1)^2 - (-1) - 2 = 1 + 1 - 2 = 0$; true.

73. (1) is false because $(\frac{-5}{3})(- \frac{3}{5}) = -1$ is false.

    Statements (2) and (3) are true for $x = - \frac{3}{5}$ as shown below.

    (2)

    $(2x - 1)(x + 5) < 2$

    $(2(- \frac{3}{5}) - 1)(- \frac{3}{5} + 5) < 2$

    $(- \frac{6}{5} - \frac{5}{5})(- \frac{3}{5} + \frac{25}{5}) < 2$

    $(- \frac{11}{5})(\frac{22}{5}) < 2$ TRUE

    (3)

    $x - \frac{1}{2} = - \frac{11}{10}$

    $- \frac{3}{5} - \frac{1}{2} = - \frac{11}{10}$

    $- \frac{6}{10} - \frac{5}{10} = - \frac{11}{10}$ TRUE

    Answer [f]

74. Statement [a] is correct because both ratios make the same comparison: the number of computers in the numerator and the number of days in the denominator. **Answer [a]**

75. The formula for area is length x width = area. If the area is held constant, then the length and width vary inversely.
$\frac{L1}{L2} = \frac{W2}{W1}$; L1 = 12, W1 = 4, W2 = 5
$\frac{12}{L2} = \frac{5}{4}$ **Answer [c]**

76. (a) shows $x \leq -1$. (b) shows $y \leq -2$. (d) shows $x \geq 0$, $y \geq 0$ and $y \leq 2$. **Answer [c]**

77. The equation of the vertical line is $x = -3$ and the shaded area to the right of the line is $(x > -3)$. The equation of the diagonal line is $x + y = -2$ and the shaded area above the line is $(x + y > -2)$. The answer must use the word "and" to obtain the intersection of the two shaded areas mentioned above. The word "or" cannot be used because it would allow the union of the two areas. **Answer [d]**

78. Trying ordered pairs that are on the graph with each equation will pinpoint the correct answer. (2,0) and (-2,0) are not solutions of (b) or (d) but they are on the graph. (4,2) and -4,2) are on the graph but not solutions of (c). **Answer [a]**

79. [a] is the only correct answer as shown by the answer to problem 78 of the Form A test.

80. Answer [c] is the closest to the school population distribution.

81. The probability that the first ball is red is $\frac{4}{9}$ because there are 4 red balls and 9 balls altogether in the sample space. After the first ball is drawn and replaced, there are still 9 balls in the sample space. Therefore the probability that the second ball is green is $\frac{3}{9}$. The probability that the first ball is red and the second ball is green is the product of the two fractions. $\frac{4}{9} \cdot \frac{3}{9} = \frac{4}{27}$ **Answer [a]**

82. The coins have 4 outcomes: HH, HT, TH and TT. Therefore the probability of obtaining exactly two tails is $\frac{1}{4}$ and the probability of not obtaining two tails is $1 - \frac{1}{4} = \frac{3}{4}$. **Answer [b]**

83. [a]

84. [e] A correct answer would be "Burt loafs and he does not fail."

85. [a]   86. [c]   87. [e]   88. [c, d]   89. [c]

90. [b]   91. [f]   92. [b]   93. [g]   94. [g]

95. [g]   96. [b]   97. [c]   98. [2]   99. [c]

100. [d]   101. [c]   102. [a]   103. [b]   104. [c]

105. [a]   106. [b]   107. [b]   108. [c]   109. [b]

110. [a]   111. [c]   112. [a]   113. [d]   114. [b]

115. The expression 2^n generates the number of outcomes if n represents the number of coins. $2^5 = 32$. [d]

116. [c]   117. [b]   118. [2]

119. They sold 45 pair and made $5.00 each. 45 x $5 = $225.00   They were charged $3 each for the 5 returned and $225 - $15 = $210.00. Answer [b]

120. Form a proportion using the ratios of the tagged deer to the total number of deer and solve using the steps below. The letter x represents the total number of deer present.

$$\frac{40}{x} = \frac{5}{20}, \quad 5x = 800, \quad \text{and} \quad x = 160 \qquad \text{Answer} \quad [d]$$

121. The numbers, 8, 13, and 18 all have a remainder of 3 when divided by 5, but only 18 is also evenly divisible by both 2 and 6.   Answer [b]

122. Use the Pythagorean Theorem to solve the problem as it applies to all right-triangle situations.

$$a^2 + b^2 = c^2$$
$$(300)^2 + (400)^2 = c^2$$
$$90000 + 160000 = c^2$$
$$250000 = c^2 \text{ and } c = 500 \text{ meters}$$

5 x $2,000 = $10,000   Answer [e]

123. 6 bundles of flooring will be needed plus the labor cost and $1,200 + $375 = $1,575   Answer [c]

124. The equipment depreciated $7,000 in ten years or $700 per year. In three years the depreciation will 3($700) or $2,100. $8,000 - $2,100 = $5,900
          Answer [b]

125. The walk forms a rectangle 23 ft. by 36 ft. with area 828 square feet. The pool has area 17 x 30 = 510 square feet and 828 - 510 = 318 sq. ft.

Answer [a]

126. To solve this inverse relation use the equation $SD^2 = k$ where S is the sound units, D is the distance, and k is a constant of proportionality. First find k when S = 2 and D = 20 as shown in the left column below.

$$2(20)^2 = k$$
$$2(400) = k$$
$$800 = k$$

Next, find S when k = 800 and D = 60 as shown on the right above.

$$S(60)^2 = 800$$
$$3600S = 800$$
$$S = \frac{2}{9}$$

Answer [b]

Note: If the sound and the distance had a direct instead of inverse relationship the equation would be $S = D^2k$.

127. Each brace wire forms the hypotenuse of a right triangle with legs of 9 meters and 40 meters. By the Pythagorean Theorem:

$$a^2 + b^2 = c^2 \quad \text{c is the hypotenuse}$$
$$9^2 + 40^2 = c^2$$
$$81 + 1600 = c^2$$
$$1681 = c^2 \quad \text{and c = 41 meters for one brace}$$
$$4 \times 41 = 164 \text{ meters total}$$

Answer [c]

128. The word sum implies that x and 5 must be added first. Therefore only (b) shows this relationship.

Answer [b]

129. (a) and (b) are both correct.

130. Eleven months is one standard deviation from the mean of 13 and the area between the mean and one standard deviation from the mean in a normal distribution is approximately 34%. Therefore the per-cent of area showing the data less than one standard deviation below the mean is 50% - 34% = 16%.

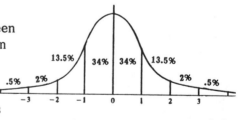

Answer [c]

131. The total number of people drops one every time a person is drawn. There-fore the probability that the first person drawn is Asian-American is $\frac{2}{18}$.

The probability that the second one is also Asian-American is $\frac{1}{17}$. For the other case, the probability that the first person drawn is Afro-American is $\frac{7}{18}$ and the second is $\frac{6}{17}$. The total probability is the sum of the two products.

Answer [a]

132. The probability $\frac{6}{7}$ shows that he can win 6 times and lose 1 out of 7 possibilities. Therefore the odds that he will <u>lose</u> the election is 1:6.   Answer [b]

133. [a, c]

APPENDIX

SCALE SCORING OF THE CLAST

The scores for the three objective subtests—computation, reading, and writing—are given three digit scores that can range from 200 (low) to 400 (high). The average scaled score for each of the subtests is given below. These can be used to compare your scores to those of other students who have taken the test. About 16% of the students will score lower than one standard deviation below the mean. Thus, 16% of the students are likely to score less than 272 on the computation test. 300 − 28 = 272 Students must pass all four portions of the test to maintain their academic standings.

Test	Mean Score	Standard Deviation
Computation	300	28
Reading	300	29
Writing	300	25

The portion of students who are likely to score above certain scores on the three subtests is given below. These figures are likely to change as more test data is obtained.

Score	Percent Scoring Above that score		
	Math	Reading	Writing
260	92%	91%	94%
270	86%	85%	88%
280	75%	74%	79%
290	63%	62%	65%
300	50%	50%	50%

ESSAY PORTION OF THE COLLEGE LEVEL ACADEMIC SKILLS TEST

The essay portion of the CLAST is the first portion presented when the test is administered. Fifty minutes is allotted to outline and write the essay. The writing chapter of this book gives further details on the writing objectives of CLAST.

After reading the explanation of the method for grading essays and the criteria for the four essay ratings, read the sample student essay that follows. It was written by William J. Boden, a St. Petersburg Junior College student. This essay received a score of "8"—a perfect score. This means that each of the two readers of his essay evaluated it with a "4" rating. Note how his essay meets the criteria of excellent organization, specific details, and few, if, any errors even though it was writen in fifty minutes simulating actual CLAST conditions.

Explanation of the Method for Grading Essays

Each essay is read by two trained readers who are using a holistic grading method. This method considers the whole essay, not just the grammar, spelling, or other items. Each reader rates an essay independently using a scale of one (lowest rating) to four (highest rating). The total score for each essay is the sum of the two ratings. Therefore the lowest score is a two $(1 + 1 = 2)$ and the highest is an eight $(4 + 4 = 8)$. A score of five indicates that one reader gave a two and the other one a three. Any essay that receives a one from only one reader is sent to a referee for rescoring. The average score for an essay is 4.7 with a standard deviation of 1.5. This means that approximately 33% of the students taking the test will score lower than 4 on the essay portion of CLAST. Approximately 42% of the students will score higher than 5 and about 20% will score higher than 6 on the essay.

Criteria for the Essay Ratings

Following are descriptions of essays that earn a 1, 2, 3, or a 4 from the trained readers. The total score for each essay is the sum of the scores given by two readers.

Ratings

1   Writer includes very little, if any, specific and relevant supporting detail but, instead, uses generalizations for support. Thesis statement and organization are vague and/or weak. Underdeveloped, ineffective paragraphs do not support the thesis. Sentences lack variety, usually consisting of a series of subject-verb and, occasionally, complement constructions. Transitions and coherence devices are not discernible. Syntactical, mechanical, and usage errors occur frequently.

2   Writer employs a limited amount of specific detail relating to the subject. Thesis statement and organization are unambiguous. Paragraphs generally follow the organizational plan, and they are usually sufficiently unified and developed. Sentence variety is minimal and constructions lack sophistication. Some transitions are used, and parts are related to each other in a fairly orderly manner. Some errors occur in syntax, mechanics, and usage.

3   Writer presents a considerable quantity of relevant and specific detail in support of the topic. The thesis statement expresses the writer's purpose. Reasonably well-developed, unified paragraphs document the thesis. A variety of sentence patterns occur, and sentence constructions indicate that the writer has facility in the use of language. Effective transitions are accompanied by sentences constructed with orderly relationship between word groups. Syntactical, mechanical, and usage errors are minor.

163

4   Writer uses an abundance of specific, relevant details, including concrete examples, that clearly support generalizations. Thesis statement effectively reflects the writer's purpose. Body paragraphs carefully follow the organizational plan stated in the introduction and are fully developed and tightly controlled. Appropriate transitional words and phrases and effective coherence techniques make the prose distinctive. Virtually no errors in syntax, mechanics, and usage occur.

Sample Student Essay – Score: 8

After reading this essay compare it with the criteria above noting the features that distinguish it from a lower scoring essay. Try to identify the thesis statement, topic sentences, and other necessary features of a good essay.

There are some important mountains to climb if a person wants to led a fulfilling life, and one of them is going to college. Men and women alike, all over the world, have determined that having a college education has many benefits. A person who is seriously considering going to college, and who is also determining the school he wants to attend, should keep in mind the facilities at the college, the reputation of the school and faculty, cost and schedules, and whether or not his goals can be met through their particular curriculum.

A college can only serve its students as well as it is capable. If a classroom has no heat in the winter, and Dr. Carl Sagan is lecturing on physics, the message is lost. This is a small example of how facilities are so important to a school's output.

164

If the athletic equipment is new, the athletes will perform better. The library should be up-to-date on all the best research books, for this is where many students will search out materials for their papers, and for the satisfaction of their own curiosity. It is easy to see that facilities are important.

Not only should a student observe the campus and its facilities beforehand, but he should do a little research regarding the school and its faculty members. Most college handbooks have a listing of where the faculty studied and to what extent they have educated themselves. There is a handbook in most bookstores across the country that lists the colleges and universities and gives all the pertinent statistics that a student would like to know about various colleges including a quality rating. After looking over tht handbook of colleges, a student should look to see how many courses are offered by the professors who have impressive degrees, and if any of their classes fit into his schedule.

Thirdly, a student must think about the never-ending problem of life--money. To attend a university that charges twenty thousand dollars a year would not be sensible for someone who flips hamburgers four hours a night. The cost per credit hour is important because the tuition bill will always come around, and it must fit within the budget. Schedules are also important to college students for someone who must work during the day had better not go to a *university that offers only day courses. The extra quality that is reflective of the college that offers day and night classes, plus one that stays within everyone's budget, is unsurpassed.*

Finally, a student must look inside himself and decide what the future holds for him. There are many schools that have a reputation for being exceptional in one or two certain fields. If a student wants to be an engineer, many colleges are great for that major. Many students have attended junior colleges and moved on to four-year schools to graduate. The junior college is a good place to work out the goals that some students aren't too sure about upon graduating from high school. The counselors on campus are a great resource for assisting students on which university the student should choose.

The college-bound person has many things to consider indeed. The facilities, faculty, and reputation of a campus are very important. Cost, scheduling, and the future that lies ahead are also on the list of things to think hard about. When a person has been around a little and has had a chance to see some of the world, it is nice to see that they have the choice here in this country to attend any college they please.

William J. Boden

St. Petersburg Junior College

Clearwater, Florida

Copy Notes

Copy Notes

Copy Notes

Copy Notes